GEORGE
SEGAL

© 1989 *Ediciones Polígrafa, S. A.*
Balmes, 54 - 08007 BARCELONA (Spain)

Adapted from Sam Hunter / Don Hawthorne
George Segal. New York: Rizzoli, 1984.

I.S.B.N.: 84-343-0569-0
Dep. Leg.: B. 17.521 - 1989 (Printed in Spain)

Printed in Spain by La Polígrafa, S. A.
Parets del Vallès (Barcelona)

SAM HUNTER

GEORGE SEGAL

EDICIONES POLÍGRAFA, S. A.

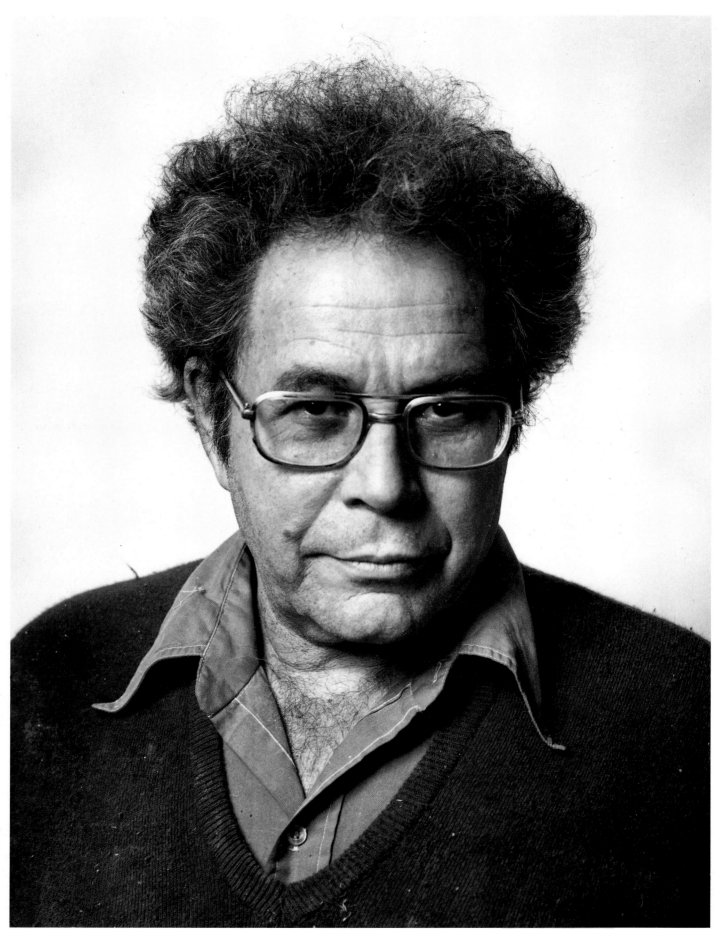

Photo: Allan Finkelman

George Segal

Segal's family background and his environment as a child were hardly the most propitious circumstances for the development of a major oeuvre in American art. Born in the Bronx in 1924 to a Jewish couple who had recently immigrated, "flat broke," from eastern Europe, Segal was never encouraged to pursue a career as an artist. "My father told me that everything was work from morning to night" — and making art, Segal remembers, was inconceivable as a worthy form of work.[1] Still, the young Segal was strongly attracted to the arts despite parental resistance, and, in his senior year at Stuyvesant High, he edited the drawings, paintings, and photographs contributed to the high school literary magazine and was awarded the Homer St. Gaudens medal for his accomplishments.

In 1941 Segal began to attend painting classes at the Cooper Union School of Art and Architecture, overcoming his parents' alarm at his choice of an artistic career. Only the year before, the Segal family had moved to South Brunswick, New Jersey, to begin an uncertain existence as chicken farmers. During the war, the business boomed. But even after the poultry market slumped, the Segals and their transplanted New York neighbors enjoyed exchanging utopian political convictions in their country setting, and their reformist and enlightened ideological convictions had an impact on Segal and his social conscience.

Between 1941 and 1946, while helping with the family farm, Segal studied at Rutgers University in North Brunswick. In 1947, he attended Pratt Institute of Design in Brooklyn, and in 1949 he earned a bachelor's degree in art education from New York University and returned to New Jersey. That year, he started a chicken farm of his own across from his parents' in South Brunswick.

Even though he continued to maintain the chicken farm until 1958, Segal's interests lay elsewhere, partly from necessity. While at New York University, he had been dazzled by the acclaim the New York School artists received, although as a slightly younger artist with different beliefs and encouraged by Hans Hofmann, he was determined to include the "real" world in his own works. More pressingly, faced with a chicken farm that did not provide for his growing family's needs, Segal had begun to teach art and English in the local high school.

When he sold the last of his chickens in 1958, Segal converted the sprawling, low-ceilinged structures that had been their coops into studios and began to explore the routes that soon would lead to his first expressive sculpture. Eager to find a way to combine painting and sculpture, and to bridge the gap between the two by bringing painting into the world of three dimensions, Segal struggled toward synthesis.

"Everybody talked about higher planes but I had no theological or logical arguments to counter this except for my intuition," he recalled.[2] "Expressions of the spirit are completely dependent on the flesh. One thing can't be submitted for the other. Both are aspects of the same thing, which is why, in the face of Abstract Expressionism, which staggered and impressed me, I felt I honestly couldn't perform without referring to my physicalness."

Segal's first crude attempts in sculpture were as emphatically physical as any heavily pigmented Willem de Kooning canvas, and as roughly constructed as the most primitive chicken coop. In the summer of 1958, after pulling apart several department store dummies to learn how they were constructed, he modeled his first plaster figure, in the form of a reclining woman, *Bas-relief: Nude* (ill. 3). The plaster was expressively built up around a bedsheet that in turn rested on a framework of lumber and chicken wire. Intrigued with the third dimension, Segal soon attempted another figure — a man with crossed arms — modeled on burlap and mounted on a door. The surfaces of these works, roughly swirled and pock-marked, recall not only the textured impasto of Abstract Expressionist painting but also the monumental, eroded forms of the postwar French sculptor Germaine Richier, whose influence Segal acknowledges.

Nothing could be more physical, even visceral, than the three-dimensional works that Segal created in the vast spaces of his sculpture studio, his former chicken coops, between 1958 and 1960, when he slapped and molded the very affordable wet plaster onto frameworks of wood, wire and coarse burlap. Eerie crosses between golems and ghosts, these crude and hulking plaster figures were shown at the Hansa Gallery, where they appeared to have materialized in real space from his bold figurative paintings on the walls behind them. In *Legend of Lot* (ill. 1), a typical sculpture/painting combination from that pivotal year, a heavy masculine form stands hunched over before a monumental composition on which equally primitive figures are scribbled and scrawled in paint.

These first sculptures look very much at home beside the figurative "new realist" improvisations of Lucas Samaras and Claes Oldenburg, and the gritty, urban appearance of much "assemblage" art. Segal's affinities with assemblage sculpture became even more obvious the following year, when he placed a stick figure — two-by-fours with hinges at the joints — on his old bicycle, *Man on a Bicycle I* (ill. 2). Although all these works possessed unmistakable energy and promise, they were as yet rather undeveloped and experimental. He was groping for a new aesthetic, and his first steps were necessarily tentative.

Even before he had discovered his signatory technique of casting figures in plaster, however, Segal's primitive, freestanding sculptures were among the most important and individualistic expressions in a rather large body of work created by many New York artists that bridged the widening gap between the Abstract Expressionistic vision, the abortive but influential episode of assemblage constructions and Pop Art. With his crude sculptural forms, preceding his patented invention of plaster figures placed in an environment of everyday objects, Segal had found an effective means of closing the distance between the abstract space of a formalist generation and a new art of psychological responses and environmental definition. After painting for more than a decade, he began at the close of the fifties to move with a courageous independence towards a more literal apprehension of space, and to reconstruct in haunting plaster shells a sense of actual life and the dynamics of human interaction.

Segal arrived at his characteristic style of casting actual human figures in plaster and reworking the shells into a plausible environmental imagery almost by chance. The momentous, if accidental, breakthrough occurred in the summer of 1961, when he taught an adult painting class in New Brunswick. The class was encouraged to make use of odd and unlikely materials in assemblages, and one woman brought to class a box of surgeon's bandages. Segal took some home with the intention of wrapping them around one of the chicken-wire frameworks he had constructed for his sculptures. Then it occurred to him to dip the cloth bandages in plaster and apply them directly to the body. He sat on a chair and instructed his wife to cover him in soaked bandages. The new technique led to a few anxious moments when the plaster began to harden, heat up, and contract, and the artist lost a good portion of his body hair in the course of frantically removing the casts. With great difficulty, he was able to reassemble the pieces into a complete figure which he then placed on a battered studio chair. Next Segal decided to provide a real environment for his plaster effigy. The chair was moved up to a table, to which was nailed an old window frame. The result, entitled *Man Sitting at a Table* (ill. 4), marked the discovery of a new sculptural technique and a turning point in the artist's career.

Almost as unsettling as the physical trauma of inventing his first cast sculpture were the philosophical implications of the figure that resulted. *Man Sitting at a Table* was not created by an artist inspired by the human form, but was taken from the living body in much the same way as fashion mannequins that had long been used commercially. But Segal's work was more serious and obviously intended as art, not as a commercial product. As such it challenged ancient taboos about the very nature of art and creation. Yet the very directness, the unavoidably mass-produced method of the new technique

Segal had stumbled upon could hardly have been more right for its time — and for the artist himself. By using common plaster to make the human body into the vehicle for molding an inert object, just as the emerging Pop artists were making the crass, disposable objects produced and used by a consumer-oriented society the subjects of their cool, critical work, Segal demonstrated the affinities between high art and readily available, nonprecious materials.

Segal's live casting methods and his environmental assemblages, with their vivid backgrounds of gas stations, coffee shops, movie marquees, billboards, neon signs and traffic signs plunged him into the mainstream of the emerging Pop Art phenomenon in the early sixties. Popular culture and a variety of mass communications had just been rediscovered as a vital art source by a diverse group of young Americans. They had been influenced to some degree by the phenomenon of assemblage, by the figural Expressionist painters and the Happenings which inventively mixed environmental flotsam with a symbolic human theater. The new generation, however, drew their imagery almost exclusively from commercial and popular entertainment sources. They also differed from their immediate forebears in their aversion to personal expressiveness, and their preference for the slick and finished advertising-world surfaces. These brash new symbols of postwar material affluence swiftly superseded the derelict and nostalgic ''junk'' effects of the assemblagists, with their evocative signs of age or use. The Pop artists fabricated an art based on a postwar consumer's paradise of gleaming new products, recognizable brand names, film and television icons, teenage romance or action comics, and the other standard visual fare of contemporary mass society. These artist were willing to stake their sensibilities on the vernacular of the market place rather than on traditional high art sources.

Segal, however, immediately differentiated himself from his generally younger colleagues in the new, populist idioms by isolating his art from their more obvious commercial styles. He differed dramatically in the psychological nuance and social depth of commentary of his unique plaster forms. His environmental staging and signs of the mass media were further mitigated by a taste for nostalgia-laden, derelict objects taken from the everyday world. The sense of a predigested visual experience screened by the second reality of the media was not the essential substance of his art. His subject matter remained insistently personal, taken from ordinary daily experiences — sometimes rather private (*Woman Shaving Her Leg*, ill. 6; or *Ruth*), and created in the voyeuristic spirit of Degas' naturalism. His vision could also be more general and even analytical, summarizing vocational roles across a broad social spectrum (*Cinema*, ill. 7; *The Dry Cleaning Store*, ill. 12), or even touching hedonistically on the world of entertainment (*Rock and Roll Combo*, ill. 13).

In the sixties Segal created editorialized stereotypes of middle- and lower-class America, drawing his materials and subjects from the immediate environment. These sculptures were not portraits of individuals but broad caricatures, often caustic, of modern society. Despite his almost classificatory sense of human activities and quick response to social status, there was no specific social message in his work, no literary commentary or polemic, no Pop ironist's implicit protest against American materialism, food habits and shallowness. The unique quality of his work was, in fact, its poetic statement, an approach in the spirit of traditional American romantic realism. His work was linked, appropriately enough, to the paintings of Edward Hopper, who was often cited in criticism as a predecessor.

As a particularly convincing example of this alienating effect, and surely one of Segal's most haunting compositions, *The Gas Station* (ill. 9) epitomizes what the critic Lawrence Alloway called the American highway subculture, with its associations of rootless wandering, personal estrangement and the loss of individual identity "on the road." The dispirited and gloomy boredom of the two figures in the gas station and their immobility have even encouraged the comparison to depersonalized mummies. Their torpor is both intentional — an effort to symbolize human introspection — and accidental, stemming from the uncanny effects Segal discovered when he commenced building sculptural forms from plaster-soaked bandages. As with the Romans of Pompeii, the gestures and routine daily movements of his actors seem arrested and fixed as if caught in a lava flow. Segal's immobilized figures, however, also function as an important foil and contrast to the revivified environmental objects of a familiar gas station scene, which in turn takes on a kind of uncanny, theatrical brilliance.

In *The Bowery* (ill. 42) Segal evinced an even more starkly poignant realism and some sense of social compassion, delineating a persuasively authentic scene with a drunken bum lying on the floor while another leans against a drab zinc and wood background, smoking a cigarette. Typical of his best genre realism are the numerous box-like compositions of the sixties with partial or full plaster figures leaning over a sleazy red restaurant table, facing a cup and saucer and their own reveries.

On the level of a more private and intimate perception of reality, Segal's *Woman Shaving Her Leg* (ill. 6) shows cunning intellect in his exploration of psychological, formal and art historical linkages even within such a familiar genre study. His heavy-set female figure has a purposely gross definition to the point of caricature, in order to dispel any lingering associations with ideal beauty or seductiveness. Like Degas, Segal here assumes the role of the rapt but cold observer who sees and records, albeit in his vivid contemporary fashion, an intensely intimate and personal world. Segal similarly enjoys the play of ironies between art and his role of the peeping-Tom, which he later, in fact, pursued in a more conscious exploitation of erotic visual stimulation.

While Segal kept the more blatant and familiar emblems of the Pop environment at bay, distancing them through the evocative poetic properties of his plaster effigies, he also learned to use some of these received images with finesse and in strikingly varied dispositions which attest to his compositional skills and invention. In *Cinema* (ill. 7) of 1963 the human figure and the fluorescent sign he is arranging attain an equivalence of emphasis. The impact of the total image essentially becomes the encounter between dissonant realities, human and mechanical, and not merely the action of placing letters on a movie marquee. Six years later, in 1969, Segal developed a series of brilliant variations around the idea of a "box" enclosure in order to frame smaller, more humanly scaled vignettes showing partial figures in action and at rest, with sections of signs or lettering, as in *Box: Man in a Bar* (ill. 34). Alternately, in the same mode he alluded to a more makeshift and homely domesticity rather than to the public, shared Pop environment, in such works as *Box: Woman Looking through Window* (ill. 35). The following year he tackled a far more ambitious context in *Times Square at Night* (ill. 41). Two lumpish young men pose in single file, moving towards the viewer and set off by a movie marquee in the background advertising pornographic films, overlaid with another competing neon sign for a pancake house. The illusion of the illuminated signs (which Segal elaborately reconstructed in a light box of colored gels and stick-on plastic letters) takes on a certain magical quality despite their sleazy references.

Segal's realist genre themes and frozen figures, depicted in moments of introspection characteristic of his art in the sixties, changed in the next decade. The young men striking out into the night against the background of the blinking lights and visual excitement of Times Square already suggested a new taste for higher energy levels and figures in movement. A variety of other urban scenes, such as *Walk, Don't Walk* (ill. 71), *The Red Light* (ill. 50), and *To All Gates* (ill. 46), and a new interest in the poetry of bodily motion and straining muscular effort in a series of acrobats, dancers and circus figures all gave more emphasis to the grace and agility of the human form rather than to the body as a symbol of physical enervation or metaphysical questioning. These changes could be ascribed at least in part to Segal's mastery of new techniques of figure construction. Beginning in 1971 he abruptly shifted from creating plaster shells, and freely modeling their surfaces, to working from a more exact and refined positive cast in hydrostone, a more durable industrial plaster taken from the original plaster matrix formed around his models.

The lyricism always underlying even the most primitive of Segal's earlier work became more insinuating when he abandoned his heavier outside casting method for the more delicate and accurate effects of inside casting. Particularly moving are two life-sized frontal fragments, *Girl in Robe I* (ill. 57) and *Girl in Robe III* (ill. 58). Like the contemporary *Girl Emerging from Tile Wall* (ill. 61) and *The Corridor* (ill. 65) of 1976, in which a nude woman painted flat blue stands between a yellow door and a red chair, the realism of every aspect of the human form is unavoidably emphasized, as are the details of any clothing the sitter might wear. Along with the new, intense association with living, breathing flesh that so resembles reality — as well as ancient and academic sculpture — Segal began to experiment with the addition of color to his pieces in 1976.

10

In *The Corridor*, a rather stark confrontation with an intensely blue female nude, the few found and invented forms are carefully arranged at specific, tense intervals. Flat primary colors appear to be applied almost programmatically. The use of the bold, flat tones against an equally flat black background expresses Segal's rather complex color theories particularly well. "The uninflected flat paint was something like a habitual hangover, a habit and carryover of 1960s painting, some of which I think is extraordinarily good, like the work of Ellsworth Kelly. And also, I have to admit the influence of Barney Newman," he said.

"I buried Barney's painting in the sculpture. There's all this history of Newman and Rothko using color — their attitudes toward color were exactly the same as Gauguin's, whose big, uninflected, flat areas of color are extensions of a psychological state of mind. So, I made a series of sculptures using color like that.

"On one level, *The Corridor* is very sensual — the door is open and welcoming. On the other hand, it's about the passage of time, and intimations of mortality," Segal wrote.[3] "Things happen that are hard to explain: trying to combine memory, formality, the literal and literary in one piece."

The same sensuality appears in such works as the dark, brooding *Couple on Black Bed* (ill. 73) of 1976, which shows a man resting on his back, resigned, while an intensely blue woman turns away from him, shoulders bowed as if in unspoken regret. "Color can be seductive, hallucinatory, depressing, disquieting, exhilarating ... can be the rise and fall of my state of mind," Segal has written.[4] "I decided to stop being furtive about this secret delight in the mid-seventies, and started painting on new work. I have gone through these color cycles at different times in my life."

While the inside casting technique inevitably gave Segal's images a far more lifelike surface, they scarcely approximated the intense realism and social narratives in polyester and fiber glass, painted with oil, of the trompe-l'œil illusionism of Duane Hanson and the later photorealists. Curiously, the increase in surface information and detail effected by the photorealists who had emerged in the late sixties eliminated the need for a relationship to a setting of actual environmental objects. Only the gallery stage was necessary, a neutral background. By contrast, the poetics and generality of Segal's humanity, and his figures' subtle tensions with their mundane surroundings created a psychic distance between the created forms and their contrived, object-laden surroundings. The dual realities allowed a sense of mystery to develop, and underscored subjective values rather than social commentary, or the distracting mechanical accuracy of photographic representation in three dimensions.

Paradoxically, Segal progressed to a freer and more expansive form of expression soon after he developed the more detailed casting process of working from inside the mold. Especially in his bas-reliefs, and in a powerful series of erotic tableaux, Segal found a new freedom in emulating Degas'

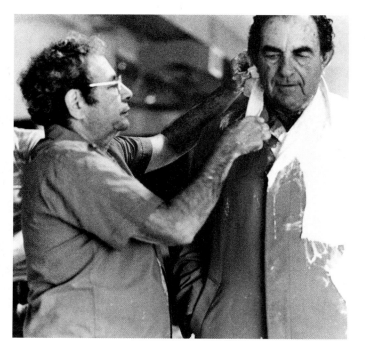 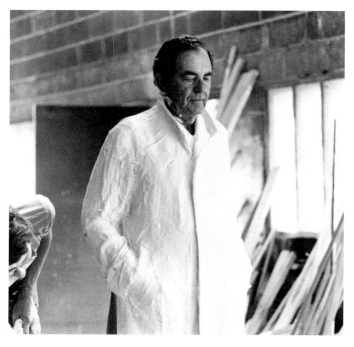

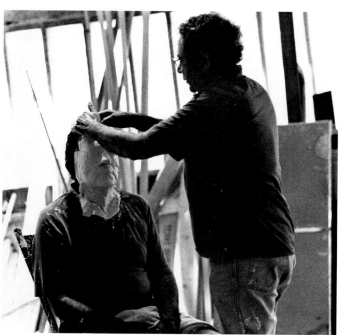 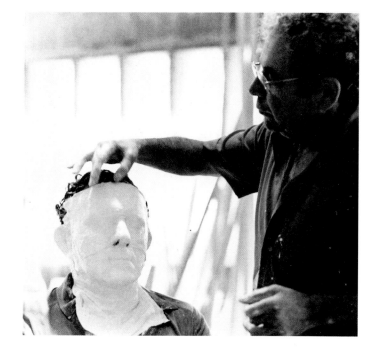

late pastels of women at their toilet, those intimately observed psychological encounters that are at the same time supremely plastic inventions. Segal's bas-reliefs often achieve an exhilarating tension, similar to Degas', between realism or descriptive function, and a far more powerful feeling for the subjects themselves, which he apparently has begun to comprehend with a new generosity of spirit, and with a force and warmth his work has never before evinced in quite the same way. He has thus moved from his early populist reconstruction of the human situation, seen in terms of contemporary culture, and from commentary on the social scene, to a concern for states

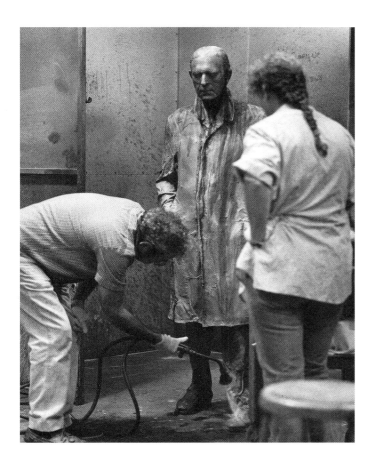

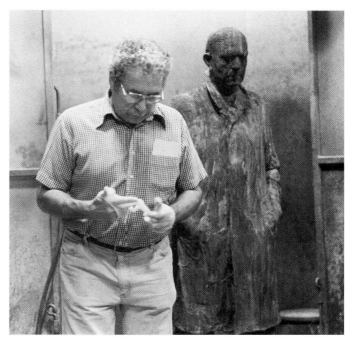

George Segal working with the model David Savage and applying finishing touches to the bronze casting of *Man in Raincoat* at Johnson Atelier foundry. Princeton, New Jersey, September, 1988. Photos by Naomi Savage.

of feeling in a broader sense. By heightening anatomical details and fragmentary anatomical forms, Segal is now able to enlarge and simplify his vision, making contact with deeper and more passionate emotions. Many of the works are in an explicitly sexual and erotic vein, and even those less charged with sensuality reveal new levels of feeling for art history.

In many of Segal's reliefs of the past two decades, and especially in such female nudes as *Girl on Blanket, Full Figure* (ill. 85) and *Red Girl on Blanket*, there are clear allusions both to classical themes and to energetic baroque composition. Mimicking classical and other traditional art forms, however, has always been an oblique aspect of his work. His search for mythical associations and for a more universal subject matter in historical art suggest that his modernity requires the foil of the past to offset the mundane surroundings of his sculpture, with its real objects and walk-through spaces. By joining his work to mainstream art history he has heightened its other preoccupation in subject matter, namely, the vulgar present and commercial culture. Playing off the past and present also has other implications. His expanded awareness of art history has the same ambivalence about it that one finds in Lichtenstein's Picasso parodies, for example, or Warhol's reconstruction in flattened, silk-screened icons of the Mona Lisa. Major figures of the Pop-art generation have often quoted the recent past in a spirit of ironic parody.

Since the mid-seventies Segal has found himself grappling with some of the disturbing dilemmas that confront the successful contemporary artist who attempts to create commissioned public sculpture under government and corporate auspices. He has often wondered out loud whether making works for public sites was not, indeed, a contradiction in terms for the modern artist committed to a private, introspective and contemplative art. Would such art survive the transition from gallery to street? Can outdoor works, deprived of the controlled space and light of the gallery, succeed aesthetically at the level of the best indoor works and make sense to an untrained and often unsympathetic audience? These were some of the questions that occurred to him, he has said, as he accepted numerous public commissions over the past decade and a half, when government patronage of the arts so notably flourished. Two of Segal's commissions in particular attracted more popular attention, and more intense controversy, than he had ever before experienced in his mature sculpture career.

Both *Kent State: Abraham and Isaac* (ill. 81) and *Gay Liberation* (ill. 89) are monuments in the traditional sense: the first commemorates a historic event; the second, the struggle for recognition of a persecuted minority. Furthermore, both works clearly succeeded in communicating their commemorative intention to the public, largely because of their figural realism. But this does not mean that *Gay Liberation* or *Kent State: Abraham and Isaac* resolved all the dilemmas of the contemporary monument. In each case, when a work's worth was debated in a public forum, discussion inevitably ignored its value as an art object and concentrated instead on the merits of the issues it memorialized.

In early September, 1978, officials of Kent State University announced that Segal's sculpture commemorating the killing of four university students on May 4, 1970, by National Guardsmen was unacceptable for exhibition on the campus. It had been eight years since the students had been shot in an antiwar demonstration that had gained national prominence and symbolic value for propagandists of the left and right. But eight years was not long enough. In a statement explaining why the university was rejecting the gift of the Cleveland-based Mildred Andrews Fund, which had commissioned the work, Robert McCoy, the executive assistant to the president, said, ''An act of violence about to be committed is inappropriate to commemorate an act of violence.'' He added, ''We were afraid it would upset the delicate balance we have here now at the university. We simply could not afford this type of art — even if someone was giving it to us.''[5]

Although Segal received support from many quarters, including the faculty and student body, the university stood firm, and the Mildred Andrews Fund withdrew its gift, which was eventually transferred to Princeton University. When the work was finally dedicated at Princeton on October 5, 1979, six of the students wounded in the Kent State shootings, and the parents of three of the four who were killed, were present. Fred Licht, the director of the

14

University Art Museum, said that the work represented a return to "the monumental origins of sculpture, the possibility it gives us to express our culture and our society. We have a good deal of first-rate twentieth century sculpture on our campus, but none has a specific relationship to the crises that contemporary students and contemporary teachers have lived with. This sculpture has a living presence that goes beyond the appeal of our other works and has a direct meaning which can hold the attention of all our students, even those who are not interested in art as such."[6]

For all the controversy surrounding it, *Kent State: Abraham and Isaac* has finally found a calm and relatively sympathetic home in Princeton; the story of *Gay Liberation* (ill. 89) has thus far no such happy ending. In 1979, Segal was asked by Peter Putnam, the administrator of the Mildred Andrews Fund, if he would be interested in executing a sculpture honoring the gay-rights movement. According to Bruce Voeller, the founder of the Mariposa Foundation, which originated the idea for the work and acted as Putnam's agent, the commission specified only that the work "had to be loving and caring, and show the affection that is the hallmark of gay people — it couldn't be ambiguous about that ... And it had to have equal representation of men and women."[7] The sculpture was to be placed in downtown Manhattan.

Following his usual procedure, Segal toured the Greenwich Village site with his wife; after viewing the proposed location at Christopher Park in Sheridan Square, he was determined to approach the subject in a manner appropriate to a neighborhood where he saw "young mothers pushing strollers." Segal has lyrically and passionately celebrated the theme of physical love throughout his career. *Gay Liberation* is the logical successor to such works as *Lovers on a Bed I* (ill. 5; 1962), and *The Girl Friends* (1969), which depicts lesbian lovers in an understated demonstration of affection. The public location of *Gay Liberation* would not permit Segal the frank celebration of sexuality and eroticism that typify many of his gallery works. Instead, he depicted two couples, one male, one female, each absorbed in a gentle, affectionate exchange that loses nothing in emotion or sensuality for all its restraint. The men are standing, one resting his hand on his partner's shoulder. The women are seated on a park bench; one tentatively holds a finger to her mouth, while the other rests a hand on her knee.

But *Gay Liberation* is not only a sensitive and perceptive social statement; it is a masterful composition in space. The two park benches in the work barely adumbrate an environmental setting, yet provide a strong horizontal that the figure groups accent like grace notes. Both couples contain strong diagonal rhythms, which balance each other and play off the intersections in the black steel of the park bench. Finally, the bench invites the spectator to join the scene, at once adapting the sculpture to its environment and domesticating a potentially threatening subject.

The work was offered as a gift to the city, but it required the approval of a gauntlet of city organizations and community groups. Despite the endorsement of Greenwich Village political leaders, including Representatives Theodore Weiss and Bella Abzug, the Village Independent Democrats, and the city's Director of Historic Parks, as well as the editorial support of the *Village Voice, Gay Liberation* encountered vocal opposition at three separate public meetings in the summer and fall of 1980.

Although *Gay Liberation* has passed reviews by the Fine Arts Commission, Community Board Two, and the Landmarks Commission, the city has never allocated the funding to install the work and provide additional landscape architecture for the park — a rider that was added in a compromise with the work's critics. Putnam's fund sponsored a second bronze for a public site in Los Angeles, but *Gay Liberation* met much the same fate in California as it had in Greenwich Village. The local government has refused to accept the work on public land; and Putnam has insisted that it be installed nowhere else. Today neither of the two bronzes have been sold, although one is on loan to Stanford University, California, and the other has been temporarily installed in a public park in Madison, Wisconsin, with the approval of city officials. The issues they addressed are thus still unresolved, insofar as they have no permanent place either in an urban or academic environment.

In the winter of 1981, perhaps seeking relief from the distractions of the unresolved and disturbing controversies that had arisen around his Kent State Memorial and Gay Liberation monuments, Segal turned directly to Cézanne for renewal and spiritual nourishment, creating a serious meditation on high art of the modernist past rather than the parody that might have been expected from an artist associated with Pop Art. Peaches appear about to roll off the side of a narrow shelf in *Cézanne Still Life No. 2* (ill. 97) and *Cézanne Still Life No. 4* (ill. 100), both astoundingly textural, illusionistic tours-de-force that wittily recall the older artist's work without detracting from Segal's achievement. Part of the work's charm comes from its referential qualities, and part from its brilliant composition. But most comes from the subtle handling of paint, rich and varied, and from the dramatic stage-like use of light and dark. Segal's exploration of a vivid, chromatic sculpture of an intensely private character gave him a well deserved respite from the pressures and extroversion of making commissioned public works. In his particular genre of art-about-art, as it might be described, Segal reconstructed in his own terms Cézanne's familiar still-life subjects as three-dimensional variants on a noble traditional theme, creating an enthralling series of free copies of some of the best-known Cézanne still lifes in museum collections. These he remade with considerable care in his own inimitable sculptural form by taking plaster molds of apples, oranges and onions, plates, pitchers and bottles and painting them in thin color washes on plaster-soaked cloth drapery. He even recreated the forward tilt of Cézanne's table surfaces, a tour-de-force of spatial condensation retranslating a depicted, illusionistic pictorial space into the physicality of sculpture. The revival of the drastically elided space of the modernist pictorial genre in terms compatible with his own poetic, realist style represented a triumphant restatement of Cézanne's elevated formal vision without sacrificing the vernacular vitality of Pop Art.

16

Segal's overt homage to Cézanne, which he more recently extended to the Cubists Picasso and Braque, is simply an outgrowth of his long-held obsession with forms that intrude into the viewer's world, combining painting and sculpture in a theatrical ensemble. In the last few years he has been working consistently with "painterly paint," Segal has stated. "In a peculiar way, it's the net result of a whole series of sculptures and reliefs that I did, first from Cézanne and then from Cubism ... I've also been doing a lot of thinking about art lately.

"Cézanne and Picasso are particular heroes of mine. My favorite artists are loaded with truthful insights that I'm comfortable with; I like an awful lot about those artists — those are the artists who attracted me to modern art in the first place. So by the time I got to Cubism, I was noticing strange things that my teachers never told me; I was looking for myself. I was looking pretty closely at Picasso and Braque, who were looking over Cézanne's shoulder and taking off from where Cézanne stopped.

"In their work, there's the whole idea of examining nature, the real world right in front of you, of analyzing it, changing it into strokes and forms that end up analyzing the basic structure of the universe — very simply, stripping away a lot of that stuff," Segal said. "It's really philosophy, it's examining the same thing that every serious book I've ever read was about. They raise the question of the mystery of consciousness."[8]

From his earliest beginnings Segal has felt himself pulled in contrary directions, towards color and form, illusionistic, pictorial space and actual space. His art has, in a sense, been formed by the resolution of that instinctive duality of vision. Around 1958 he stopped painting to make sculpture because he was "hungry for something hard-edged and hard-structured. That wave lasted for me more than ten years," Segal noted. He used brilliant primary colors in his sculpture as early as *The Costume Party* (ill. 49; begun in 1965) but found that colors "made the solid ground shift under my feet — and began to touch terror, hallucination. It was much the same color I used in my paintings and pastels, with all my memories of sensual, luxurious delight."

He gave a rapid inventory of the visual effects and associations produced by color: "The Corridor: blue girl, red chair, yellow door, black room. Big, uninflected, flat areas of color as exact extensions of psychological states of mind." He continued: "Late Monet gardens at Giverny, more like Delacroix? Music, mysteries and transparencies, ambiguities of nature? Are they different from the terror and light of internal landscape?"

Finally, Segal declared: "I found myself rereading Old Master paint recipes, delighting in building transparent layers of stain on raw gesso plaster, every square inch packed and interesting."[9]

The formal problems of his sculpture resolved, Segal continued to explore questions of color and light in the work of the late 1970s and the 1980s. The deep green of a single door panel and the vibrant magenta of the plump nude posing before it clash alarmingly in a 1977 work, *Magenta Girl on Green Door* (ill. 75), but the blues and flesh tones are muted and mottled in another work of the same year, *Girl Sitting on Bed with Bedpost* (ill. 78), as are the hues in a remarkable fragment from 1978, *Hand on Right Buttock*. Segal's interest in social concerns resulted in his controversial 1980 *Gay Liberation* (ill. 89) and the somber study of an isolated shopper, the 1980 *Blue Girl on Park Bench* (ill. 92), but a number of graceful works that look back to the masters were also created, among them a reworking of the "three graces" theme with Renoiresque figures, the 1980 *Three Bathers with Birch Tree* (ill. 99), and the brooding fragment *Blue Girl in Blue Wicker Chair* (ill. 86).

Issues of color and light and dark have become increasingly important to Segal. In his most recent works, color, often in subdued hues, continued to play a dramatic emotional and psychological role. All the sculptures were a muted gray in the exhibition that followed the death of the artist's mother, and he has been examining the way such recent masters as Picasso and Braque used hue as well as chiaroscuro, much in the same spirit as he studied the way Cézanne and earlier artists achieved their effects of volume and mood through modeling.

People have called the two major Cubists "clones," Segal has said. But to him, the differences are clear. Braque wanted his works to be flat, while Picasso worked toward an almost Renaissance illusion of depth. "No matter what he did, Picasso always looked like he was trying to be a Renaissance man — his works seem to be three-dimensional, with the light coming from the upper-left-hand corner. He was working like an old master who could draw as well as Raphael, although his light was Rembranesque."

"Noticing the fine difference made him focus on light and dark, on the mysteries of chiaroscuro," Segal said. "Picasso, with his razzle-dazzle footwork, could make a Cubist drawing in the morning and a chiaroscuro drawing in the afternoon ... So I had to go back to the origin of chiaroscuro, to Leonardo's *sfumato*, with its forms emerging from darkness.

"All those connections started coming into play, and then it dawned on me that this is the twentieth century, in our time, and that I'm allowed somehow to get on a ladder and aim a light at my sculpture — I can use chiaroscuro to help define my sculpture. A photographer is allowed to use light and dark. The movies are allowed to use light and dark. But it's been forbidden territory to artists and I'm wondering why."[10]

According to Segal, the line from Caravaggio and Rembrandt, with their apparently naturalistic but actually contrived and theatrical use of light to define a painting, leads straight to modernism and to his own highly personal work: "The strange thing about modern art is that it's not public art that celebrates the power of a king or dictator; it's an intimate reflection into the minds of ordinary people, who are, somehow, valuable," he recently declared.[11]

In important ways, Segal's recent works are very much in keeping with his first sculptures. Like the works of the early 1960s, such complex tableaux as *The Expulsion* (ill. 123) of 1987 and *The Street* (ill. 125), of the same year, incorporate plaster figures cast from models with such naturalistic, typical surroundings as cliff walls and storefronts. The actors in Segal's mythical or everyday dramas continue to move with dignity — and with appropriate, believable agony or ennui. As in such groundbreaking early works as the 1961 *Man Sitting at a Table* (ill. 4) or the more ambitious but equally evocative *The Gas Station* (ill. 9) of 1963-64, the frozen figures appear to take part in some mysterious, compelling performance that can be understood but never shared. Forever outside the action, the viewer becomes the casual, unwitting witness to a moment that might be pivotal to human history — the casting of Adam and Eve from the Garden of Eden, say — or merely yet another lost soul stumbling down an urban alley, going who knows where.

In the nearly three decades that Segal's ghostly sculptures have performed their assigned rituals, they have been objects of wonder. Life-sized yet instantly distinguishable from reality because of their rough plaster surfaces and monochromatic or painterly surfaces, they nevertheless seem ready to serve the same purpose as Cycladic or archaic Greek ceremonial statuettes. They make overt, joyous references to their exalted antecedents, from lyrical sculptures on the Acropolis to Renaissance reliefs and even, to name just a few of Segal's most admired artists, to the richly shaded heroes of Rembrandt's prints and the shifting planes of Cubist studies by Picasso and Braque.

Segal's keynote compositions consistently have served to illustrate his desire to meld the separate realms of painting and sculpture, whether in such relatively crude, groping efforts of the early 1960s as *Man Leaning on a Car Door* (ill. 8), in which a deep blue backdrop frames the man and his vehicular attribute, or in the far more sophisticated *The Expulsion* of twenty-three years later, where the dejected figures of Adam and Eve trudge toward a blasted tree trunk, a wall of roaring flames separating them forever from the gates of paradise. Even in his 1988 public sculpture in downtown Trenton, *The Constructors* (ill. 113), the sketchy skeleton of I-beams that supports the figures of three hard-hatted workers serves as an effective painterly device.

Today, Segal's art may be as sensual as the overtly erotic, Boucher-like *Nude on Redwood Chaise* (ill. 112) of 1985 or as formally and psychologically compelling as *The Expulsion* of 1987, where the flames of the angel's sword block the father and mother of mankind in a pictorial extravaganza quite as awesome as any medieval hell's mouth. With the assured mastery and confidence of his later years, what particularly engages the artist today is the challenge of combining disparate or once taboo elements into a work of art.

"For years I've liked the idea of making an environment, by taking sculpture off the pedestal and being able to walk into it — it's a literal Cubism for me. I can walk around it and see the same thing from different points of view," Segal recently said.

He also feels free to introduce theatrical methods into his work and to choose from a staggering variety of late twentieth-century of materials — anything from plaster and fabric to bronze, he has said. "And I want to reintroduce narrative and have it coexist next to very strong abstract sculpture — the whole idea is to pull all of those threads together. I still love painting; I love painting on a flat surface.

"I can leave the sculptures white, and the works look perfectly good — pure or whatever. But the minute I put on the first stroke, whether it's color or black or gray, I change the experience of the sculpture, and it keeps changing."

His goal is to create a "marriage between geometric abstraction and realistic form, plus a complex mythology, plus a whole set of personal values and a stance of where you hold yourself in the world. That is important. That's where art should be going. I'm interested in tearing things apart, but I am also interested in putting things together."

Segal makes a consciously bourgeois and banal art, dealing with everyday problems and meanings, even when his form is biblical narrative, ancient myth or allegory. *Abraham's Farewell to Ishmael* (ill. 124) has a modern resonance in its drama of conflict, and in historical and contemporary fact, too, with its allusions to the foundations of Judaism and Islam. Segal's domestic dramas have the cutting edge of moral authority, and his mythologies translate into living theater. Speaking of the human dilemmas and inferred actions of his dramatis personae, he says: "These are all things that happen in ordinary people's lives, that are temporarily but deeply felt. ... Can you think of anyone who is immune? Domestic drama is really tempestuous stuff!"[12]

NOTES

1. Sam Hunter and Don Hawthorne, *George Segal* (New York: Rizzoli, 1984, p. 9.
2. Martin Friedman and Graham Beal, *George Segal: Sculptures* (Minneapolis, Minn.: Walker Art Center, 1979), p. 10.
3. Hunter and Hawthorne, p. 55.
4. Jan van der Marck, *George Segal* (New York: Harry N. Abrams, Inc., 1979), p. 222.
5. Hunter and Hawthorne, p. 99.
6. Hunter and Hawthorne, p. 102.
7. Hunter and Hawthorne, p. 104.
8. Unpublished interview with author, August, 1988.
9. Interview.
10. Interview.
11. Interview.
12. Interview.

CHRONOLOGY

1924 Born November 26 in New York City.

1930-40 Attends Public School 70 in the Bronx and Stuyvesant High School in Manhattan.

1940 Moves with family to South Brunswick, New Jersey; family begins chicken farming.

1941-42 Studies in the foundation art course at Cooper Union School of Art and Architecture, New York City.

1942 Returns to work on farm when older brother drafted.

1942-46 Studies part-time at Rutgers University, North Brunswick, New Jersey, attending courses in psychology, literature, history, and philosophy.

1946 Marries Helen Steinberg, April 7.

1947-48 Studies at Pratt Institute of Design, Brooklyn, New York.

1948-49 Studies at New York University; graduates with BA in Art Education; teachers include William Baziotes and Tony Smith; frequents the Eighth Street Club.

1949-58 Operates a chicken farm on Davidson's Mill Road in Middlesex County, New Jersey, across the road from his parents' farm.

1950 His son Jeff born.

1953 Befriends Allan Kaprow; daughter Rena born.

1956-59 Spends several weeks each summer at artists' community in Provincetown, Massachusetts; meets Hans Hofmann.

1956 First one-man show, at the Hansa Gallery, New York City.

1957 Second one-man show at the Hansa; also participates in a group show, "The New York School, Second Generation," at the Jewish Museum; Kaprow stages his first Happening at the farm.

1957-58 Teaches English at Jamesburg High School to avoid bankruptcy.

1958 Stops chicken farming; begins to experiment in sculpture; one-man shows at Hansa and at Rutgers University.

1958-61 Teaches industrial arts at Piscataway High School.

1959 One-man show at Hansa in February includes first plaster figures; serves as acting director during closing of Hansa; moves to Reuben Gallery, New York City; participates in group show at Reuben and in Whitney Museum's Annual Exhibition of Contemporary Art.

1960 Participates in group show at Reuben; moves to Richard Bellamy's Green Gallery, New York City; one-man show at Green includes first plaster figures with environments; Robert Frank films *The Sin of Jesus* at the farm.

1961-63 Enrolled in MFA program at Rutgers University; earns degree with a thesis on his own work and exhibition of his sculptures at Douglas College.

1961-64 Teaches art at Roosevelt Junior High School.

1962 One-man show at Green Gallery includes first life casts; participates in "New Realists" shows at Sidney Janis Gallery, New York City, and at Pace Gallery, Boston.

1963 One-man shows at Green Gallery; Ileana Sonnabend Gallery, Paris; and Schmela Gallery, Dusseldorf.

1964 Last one-man show at Green Gallery; begins to devote himself entirely to art.

1965-82 Begins to exhibit regularly with Sidney Janis Gallery, New York City.

1966 Executes first bas-relief.

1968-69 Lecturer in sculpture, Creative Arts Department, Princeton University, Princeton, New Jersey. One-man show at the Museum of Contemporary Art, Chicago.

1969 Executes first fragments. One-man shows at Princeton University, New Jersey, and Galerie Darthea Speyer, Paris.

1970 Receives honorary doctorate from Rutgers University. One-man show at the Wester Gallery, Western Washington State College, Bellingham.

1971 Produces *The Dancers*, sculpture in bronze. Tour (1971-73) to museums in major European cities, including Zurich, Rotterdam, Paris, and Brussels.

1976 Sent by State Department on a cultural exchange program to Soviet Union; executes first public sculpture, *The Restaurant*, installed in the Federal Office Building, Buffalo, New York.

1978 Shown in major retrospective exhibition: Walker Art Center, Minneapolis, Minnesota; San Francisco Museum of Modern Art; and Whitney Museum of American Art.

1979 Begins two important public commissions: *In Memory of May 4, 1970, Kent State: Abraham and Isaac*, later rejected by Kent State University after much public controversy; and *Next Departure* for The Port Authority of New Jersey and New York. One-man shows at Hope Makler Gallery, Philadelphia, Pennsylvania, and Serge de Bloe Gallery, Brussels.

1980 One-man show at Sidney Janis Gallery.

The Steelmakers commissioned by the Youngstown Area Arts Council and installed in urban renewal district of Youngstown, Ohio.

Kent State Memorial, commissioned by the Mildred Andrews Fund, is accepted by Princeton University and installed on the campus.

Several one-man shows in U.S. galleries and one at the Gatodo Gallery, Tokyo, Japan.

1982 One-man show at the Sidney Janis Gallery.

Large retrospective exhibition at the Seibu Museum of Modern Art, Tokyo, and exhibitions in several Japanese cities.

The Commuters installed at the Port Authority Bus Terminal, New York City.

1983 The *Holocaust* commissioned and installed in San Francisco under the auspices of the Committee for a Memorial to the Six Million Victims of the Holocaust.

Gay Liberation monument, commissioned by the Mildred Andrews Fund, is installed in Sheridan Square, Manhattan, after lengthy public dispute.

Retrospective exhibition at the Israel Museum, Jerusalem, Israel. One-man shows at the National Museum of Art, Osaka, Japan; Lowe Art Museum, Miami, Florida; and the Jewish Museum, New York City.

Continues to live and work in South Brunswick, New Jersey.

1984 One-man shows at Sidney Janis Gallery; Evelyn Aimis Fine Art, Toronto; Hope Makler Gallery, Philadelphia, Pennsylvania; and Il Ponte Gallery, Rome.

1985 One-man shows at the Galerie Esperanza, Montreal, and at Galerie Maeght-Lelong, Paris.

George Segal: The Drawings exhibition presented at the Butler Institute of American Art, Youngstown, Ohio; and *George Segal: The Holocaust* presented at the Jewish Museum, New York City.

The Constructors was commissioned by the State of New Jersey to be install in the New Department of Commerce Building, Trenton, NJ.

1986 One-man shows at the Sidney Janis Gallery and at the Galerie Brusberg, Berlin.

1987 One-man shows at the Galerie Esperanza, Montreal, and at the Richard Gray Gallery, Chicago.

1988 One-man shows at the Yares Gallery, Scottsdale, Arizona, and at the Sidney Janis Gallery, New York City.

BIBLIOGRAPHY

Books

Amaya, Mario. *Pop Art... And after.* New York: The Viking Press, 1965.

Beardsley, John. *Art in Public Places.* Washington: Partners for Liveable Places, 1981, pp. 71, 72. Detailed information on the installation of the *Steelmakers* in Youngstown.

Calas, Nicolas, and Elena. *Icons and Images of the Sixties.* New York: E.P. Dutton, 1971.

Compton, Michael. *Pop Art.* London: Hamlyn, 1970.

Hunter, Sam. *American Art of the Twentieth Century.* New York: Harry N. Abrams, 1972.

Hunter, Sam / Don Hawthorne. *George Segal.* New York: Rizzoli, 1984.

Kreytenberg, Gert. *George Segal: Ruth in Her Kitchen.* Stuttgart: Philipp Reclam Jun., 1970.

Lützeler, Heinrich. "Kunst und Literatur um 1960. Drei Stücke aus der Sammlung Ludwig: George Segal, Das Restaurant Fenster, 1967," *Festschrift für Gert von der Osten.* Cologne: DuMont Schauberg, 1970.

Marck, Jan van der. *George Segal.* New York: Harry N. Abrams, 1975. This substantial treatment of Segal's œuvre features lengthy discussions of many major works and generously proportioned illustrations. Van der Marck's emphasis on formal analysis and art historical categorization provide important and original insights, but at the expense of a balanced account of the literary, allusive, and humanistic aspects of the artist's work.

Seitz, William C. *Segal.* New York: Harry N. Abrams, 1972. This early heavily biographical monograph has been largely superannuated by more recent publications.

Thalacker, Donald. *The Place of Art in the World of Architecture.* New York: Chelsea House Publishers, 1980. Includes a thorough account of the commission and execution of *The Restaurant*, Segal's first public sculpture.

Tuchman, Phyllis. *George Segal.* New York: Abbeville Press, 1983.

Catalogues

Backlin-Landman, Hedy. *George Segal.* Princeton, New Jersey: The Art Museum, Princeton Unversity, 1969.

Barrio-Garay, José. *George Segal: Environments.* Baltimore: The Baltimore Museum of Art, 1976. Some interesting literary elucidations of the iconography in Segal's tableaux, couched in the argot of semiotics.

The Private World of George Segal. Milwaukee: Art History Galleries, The University of Wisconsin-Milwaukee, 1973. Sometimes extravagant, often enlightening, literary interpretations of Segal's œuvre.

Carey, Martin. *The New American Realism*, Worcester: Worcester Art Museum, 1965.

Courtois, Michel, and Allan Kaprow. *Segal.* Paris: Galerie Ileana Sonnabend, 1963.

Friedman, Martin. *Figures/Environments.* Minneapolis: Walker Art Center, 1970.

George Segal. Paris: Galerie Darthea Speyer, 1969.

Friedman, Martin and Graham W. J. Beal. *George Segal: Sculptures.* Minneapolis: Walker Art Center, 1978. Issued in conjunction with Segal's retrospective exhibition, this volume is properly synthetic and comprehensive. Includes a survey of the artist's career by Friedman, a discussion of influences of and relationships to other artists by Beal, and commentaries on six works by the artist.

Geldzahler, Henry. "George Segal," in *Recent American Sculpture.* New York: The Jewish Museum, 1964. A brief elucidation of Segal's early career, elegantly phrased.

Glenn, Constance W. *George Segal: Pastels 1957-1965.* Long Beach: The Art Galleries, California State University, Long Beach, 1977. An enlightening examination of Segal's undeservedly neglected pastels, including forty-four fine plates.

Kelder, Diane. *George Segal/Blue Jean Series.* New York: Staten Island Museum, 1978. The only exhibition devoted to Segal's experiments in etching.

Marck, Jan van der. *George Segal.* Zurich: Kunsthaus, 1971.

"George Segal," *Eight Sculptors: The Ambiguous Image.* Minneapolis: Walker Art Center, 1966.

George Segal: 12 Human Situations. Chicago: Museum of Contemporary Art, 1968. Includes documentation of all Segal's sculpture to date.

Pincus-Witten, Robert. "George Segal," On *Dine Oldenburg Segal: Painting/Sculpture.* Toronto: Art Gallery of Ontario, 1967.

White on White. Chicago: Chicago Museum of Modern Art, 1971. The author includes Segal, rather unconvincingly, in a discussion of the "utopian monochromism of our age."

Rauth, Emily S. *7 for 67: Works by Contemporary American Sculptors.* Saint Louis: City Art Museum of Saint Louis, 1967.

Schwartz, Ellen. *Sculpture in the 70's: The Figure.* New York: Pratt Institute, 1980.

PUBLIC COLLECTIONS

The Museum of Modern Art, New York City
The Whitney Museum of American Art, New York City
National Collection of Fine Arts, Smithsonian Institution, Washington, D.C.
Moderna Museet, Stockholm, Sweden
Albright-Knox Art Gallery, Buffalo, NY
Stedelijk Museum, Amsterdam, The Netherlands
Museum of Modern Art, Teheran, Iran
The Solomon R. Guggenheim Museum, New York City
Philadelphia Museum of Art, PA
Musée National d'Art Moderne, Beaubourg, Paris, France
Birmingham Museum of Fine Art, AL
Cleveland Museum of Art, OH
Art Institute of Chicago, and Mr. & Mrs. Frank G. Logan Collection, Chicago, IL
Art Gallery of Ontario, Toronto, Canada
Walker Art Center, Minneapolis, MN
The National Gallery of Canada, Ottawa
Mint Museum, NC
Newark Museum, NJ
Milwaukee Art Center, WI
San Francisco Museum of Art, CA
Museum Boymans-van Beuningen, Rotterdam, The Netherlands
Von Der Heydt-Museum, Wuppertal, Turmhof, Germany
Wallraf-Richartz Museum, Cologne, Germany
Hessisches Landesmuseum, Darmstadt, Germany
Weatherspoon Gallery, University of North Carolina
Kaiser Wilhelm Museum, Krefeld, Germany
Vancouver Art Gallery, Canada
New Jersey State Museum, Trenton
City Art Museum of St. Louis, MI
Detroit Institute of Art, MI
Staatsgalerie Stuttgart, Stuttgart, Germany
Kunsthaus Zurich, Switzerland
Akron Art Institute, OH
Wadsworth Atheneum, Hartford, CT
Indiana University Museum of Art, Bloomington, IN
Art Museum of the Atenaeum, Helsinki, Finland
Joslyn Art Museum, Omaha, NB
Stadtische Galerie im Lenbachhaus, Munich, Germany
Des Moines Art Center, IA
The Pennsylvania Academy of the Fine Arts, Philadelphia
Tel Aviv Foundation for Literature & Art, Mann Auditorium, Israel
Carnegie Institute, Museum of Art, Pittsburgh, Pennsylvania

Neue Galerie der Stadt, Aachen, Germany
Dartmouth College, Museum of Art, Hanover, NH
San Francisco Museum of Modern Art, CA
Neuberger Museum, Purchase, NY
Metropolitan Museum of Art, New York City
The Museum of Modern Art, Seibu Takanawa, Karuizawa, Japan
Hirshhorn Museum & Sculpture Garden, Smithsonian Institution, Washington, DC
Centre National d'Art Contemporain, Paris, France
Hudson River Museum, Yonkers, NY
Tamayo Museum, Mexico City, Mexico
Huntington Art Gallery, University of Texas at Austin, TX
Westdeutsche Spielbanken, Munich, Germany
White Memorial Museum, San Antonio, TX
Israel Museum, Jerusalem
Columbus Museum of Art, OH
Portland Museum of Art, OR
Suermondt Museum, Aachen, Germany
Seattle Museum of Art, WA
John B. Putnam, Jr. Memorial Collection, Princeton University, NJ
Staatsgalerie Moderner Kunst, Munich, Germany
Gatodo Gallery, Tokyo, Japan
Tokyo Central Museum, Japan
Shiga Museum of Art, Japan
The National Gallery of Art, Washington, DC
Cuyahoga County Justice Center, Cleveland, OH
Youngstown Area Arts Council, OH
Port Authority of New York and New Jersey
Seventh and Chestnut Associates, Philadelphia, PA
Virlane Foundation, New Orleans, LA
Des Moines Register & Tribune Company, IA
Bayerische Staatsgemaldesammlungen, Munich, Germany
Musée d'Art Contemporain, Montreal, Canada
City of Greenwich, CT
Pepsico Sculpture Garden, Purchase, NY
Museo de Arte Contemporáneo, Caracas, Venezuela
Fukuoka Municipal Museum of Art, Japan
Stadtische Kunsthalle Mannheim, Germany
Gewebesammlung der Stadt Krefeld, Germany
State of New Jersey, Department of Commerce Building, Trenton
Orton Park, City of Madison, WI, from Mildred Andrews Fund through the Madison Art Center

ILLUSTRATIONS

1. *Legend of Lot*. 1958.
   Oil on canvas, plaster, wood and chicken wire,
   72 × 96 in. (183 × 244 cm).
   Collection of the artist.

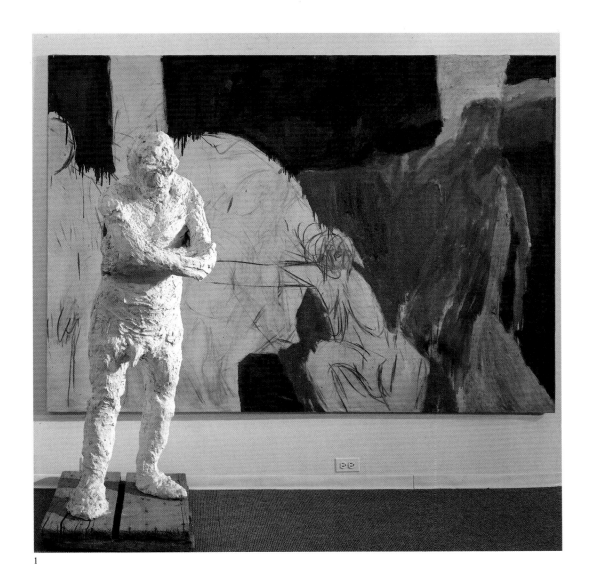

1

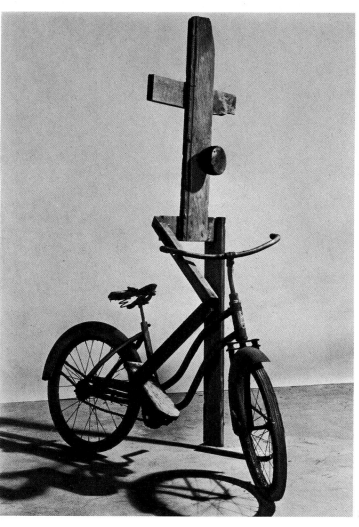

2

2. *Man on a Bicycle I*. 1958-1959.
   Wood, metal and rubber,
   65 × 58 × 24 in. (165 × 147 × 71 cm).
   Collection of the artist.

3. *Bas-relief: Nude*. 1958.
   Plaster, 36 × 66 × 3 in. (91 × 167 × 7.5 cm).
   Collection of the artist.

4. *Man Sitting at a Table*. 1961.
   Plaster, wood and glass,
   53 × 48 × 48 in. (135 × 122 × 122 cm).
   Städtische Kunsthalle Mannheim, Germany.

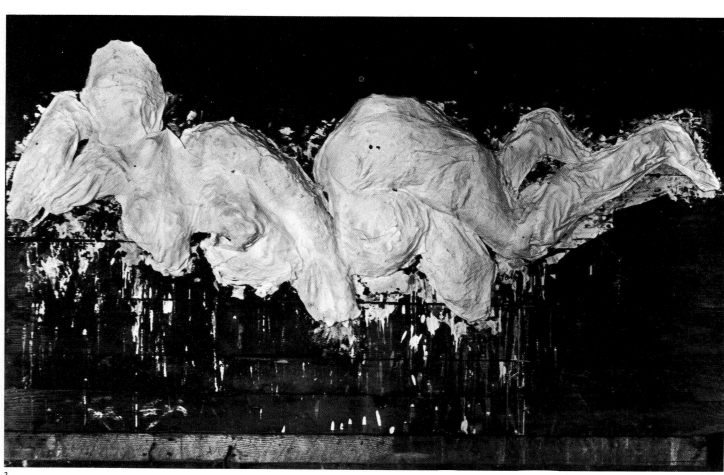

3

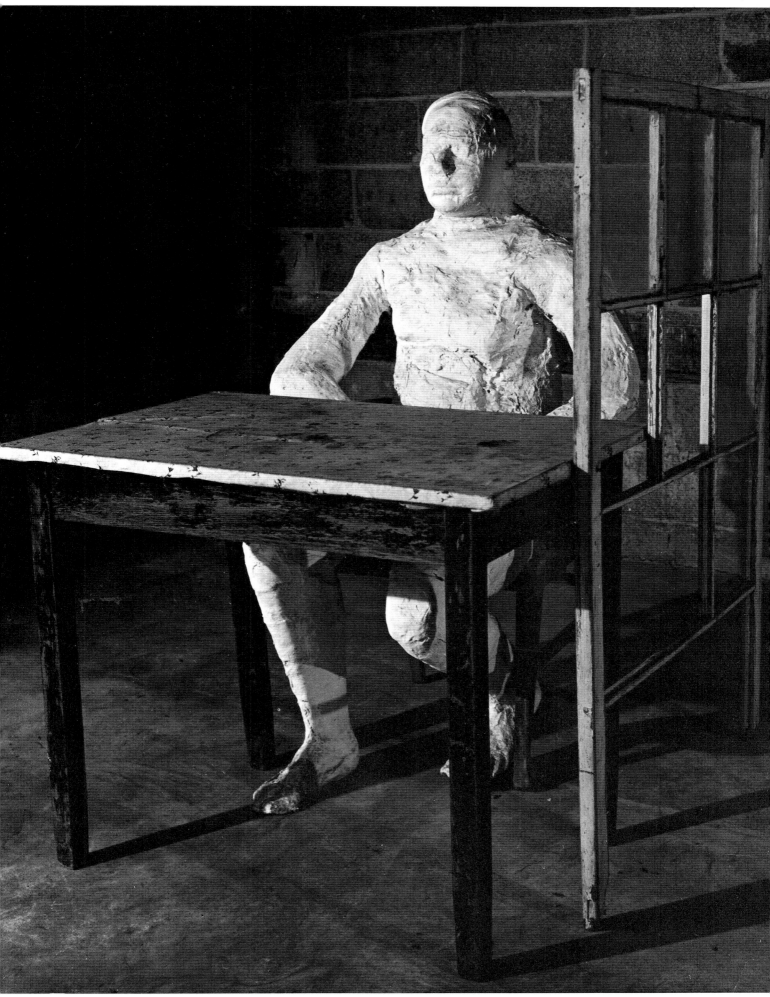

5. *Lovers on a Bed I*. 1962.
   Plaster, wood, metal, mattress and cloth,
   48 × 54 × 70 in. (122 × 137 × 178 cm).
   Collection of Mrs. Robert B. Mayer, Chicago.

6. *Woman Shaving Her Leg*. 1963.
   Plaster, metal, porcelain and Masonite,
   63 × 65 × 30 in. (160 × 165 × 76 cm).
   Collection of Mrs. Robert B. Mayer, Chicago.

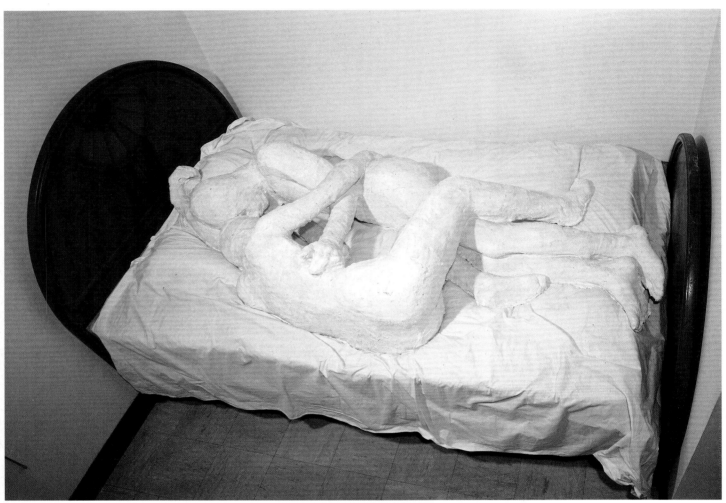

5

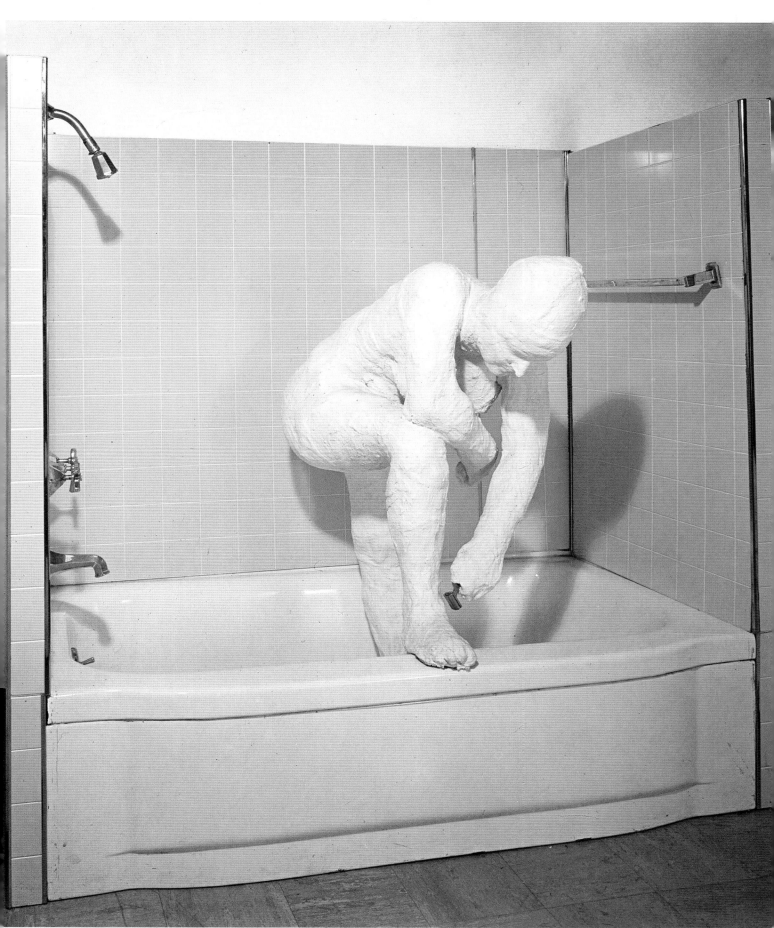

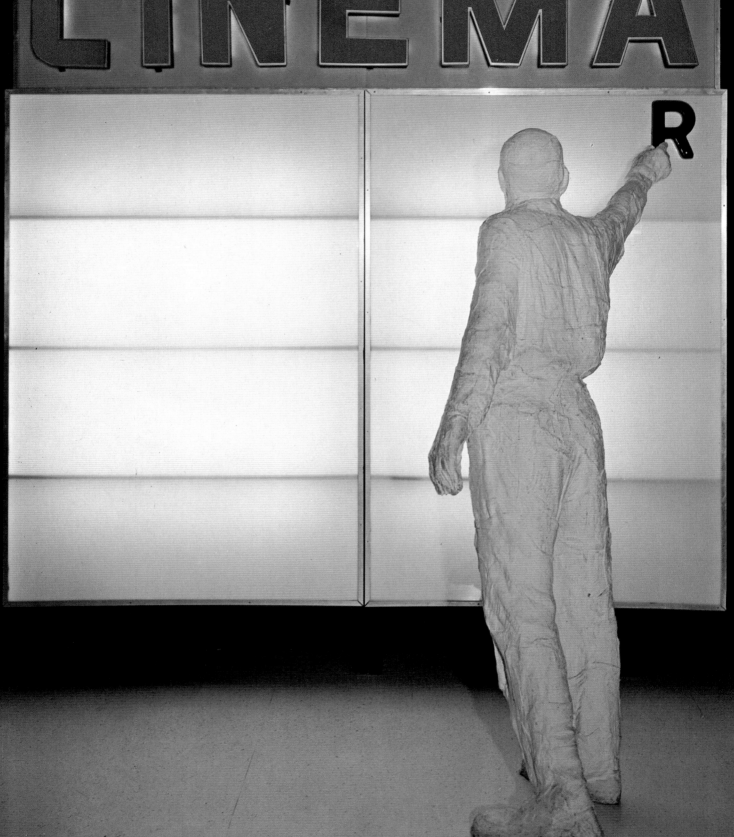

7. *Cinema*. 1963.
   Plaster, metal, Plexiglas and fluorescent light,
   118 × 96 × 39 in. (300 × 244 × 99 cm).
   Albright-Knox Art Gallery, Buffalo (Gift of Seymour H. Knox).

8. *Man Leaning on a Car Door*. 1963.
   Plaster, wood and metal,
   96 × 48 × 30 in. (244 × 122 × 76 cm).
   Staatsgalerie Stuttgart, Stuttgart.

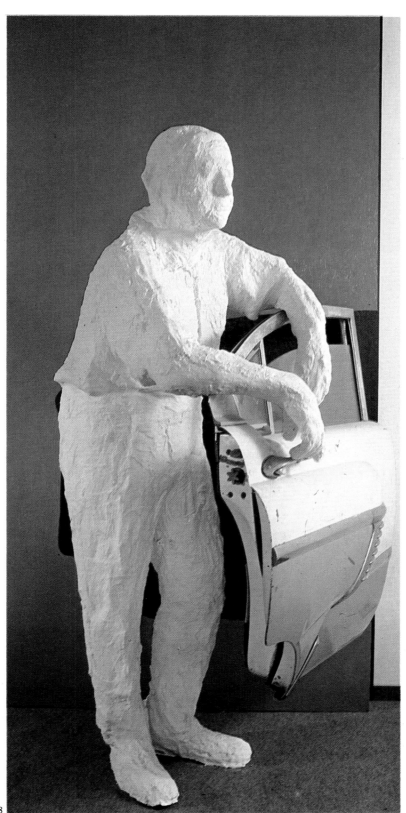

9. *The Gas Station*. 1963-1964.
   Plaster, metal, glass, stone and rubber,
   96 × 264 × 60 in. (244 × 671 × 152 cm).
   The National Gallery of Canada, Ottawa.

9

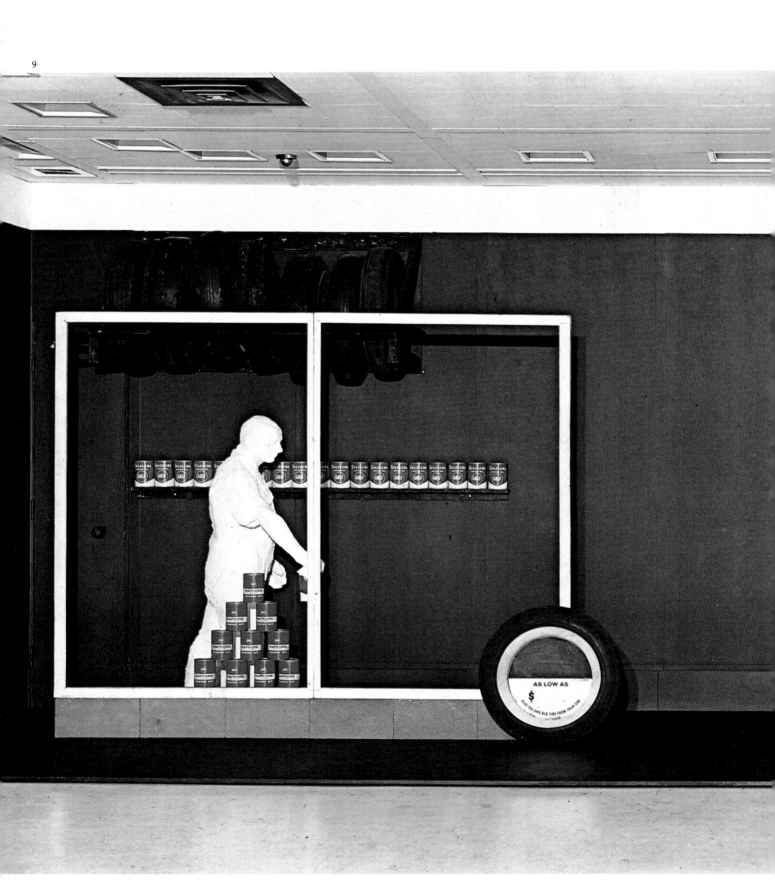

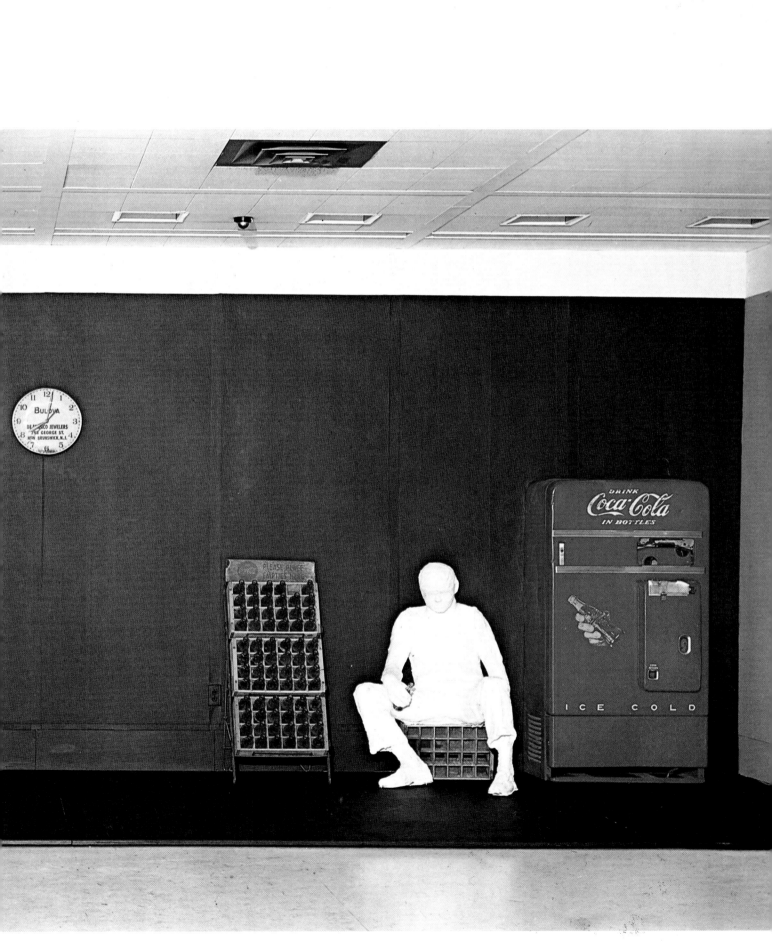

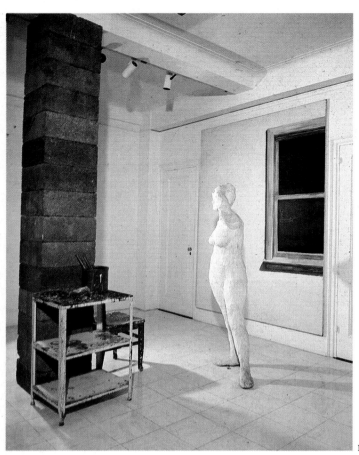

10. *The Artist's Studio*. 1963.
Plaster, wood, metal, paint and mixed media,
96 × 72 × 108 in. (244 × 183 × 274 cm).
Harry N. Abrams Family Collection, New York.

11. *The Bus Station*. 1965.
Plaster, wood an plastic,
96 × 48 × 24 in. (244 × 122 × 61 cm).
Collection of Howard and Jean Lipman, New York.

12. *The Dry Cleaning Store*. 1964.
Plaster, wood, metal, aluminum paint and neon tubing,
96 × 108 × 86 in. (244 × 274 × 218 cm).
Moderna Museet, Stockholm.

10

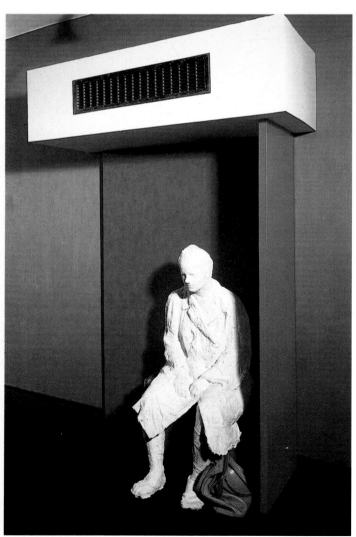

11

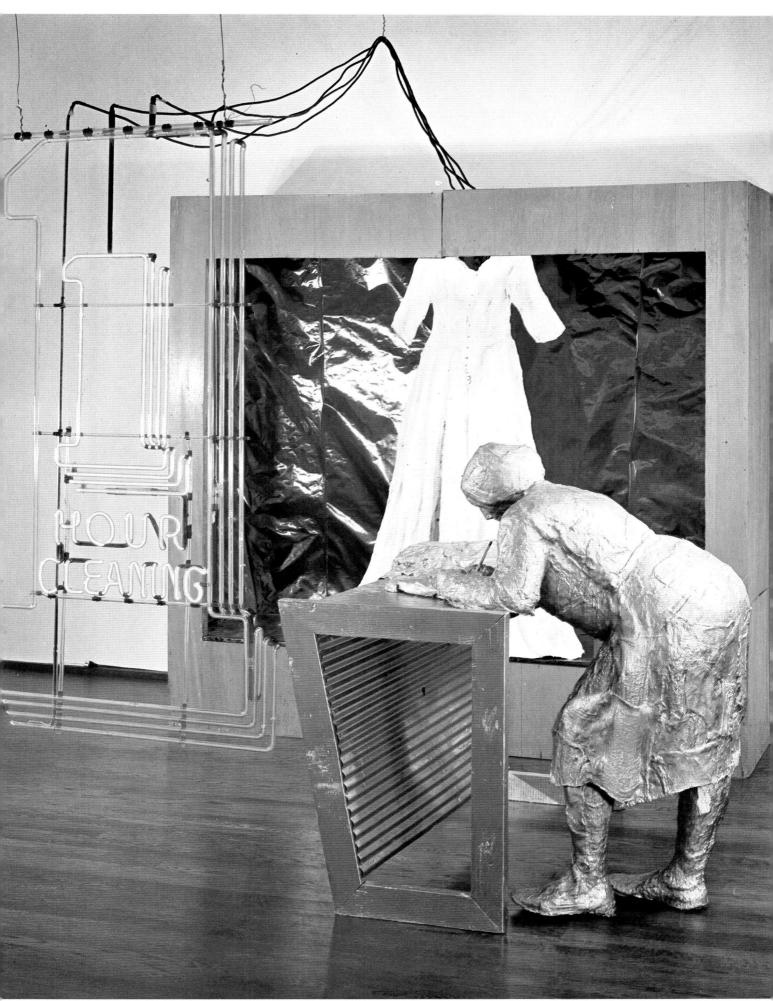

13. *Rock and Roll Combo*. 1964.
   Plaster, wood, tiling and musical instruments,
   84 × 84 × 69 in. (213 × 213 × 175 cm).
   Hessisches Landesmuseum, Darmstadt, Germany
   (Collection of Karl Stroher).

14. *Woman in a Doorway I*. 1964.
   Plaster, wood, glass and aluminum paint,
   113 × 63¼ × 18 in. (287 × 161 × 46 cm).
   Whitney Museum of American Art, New York.

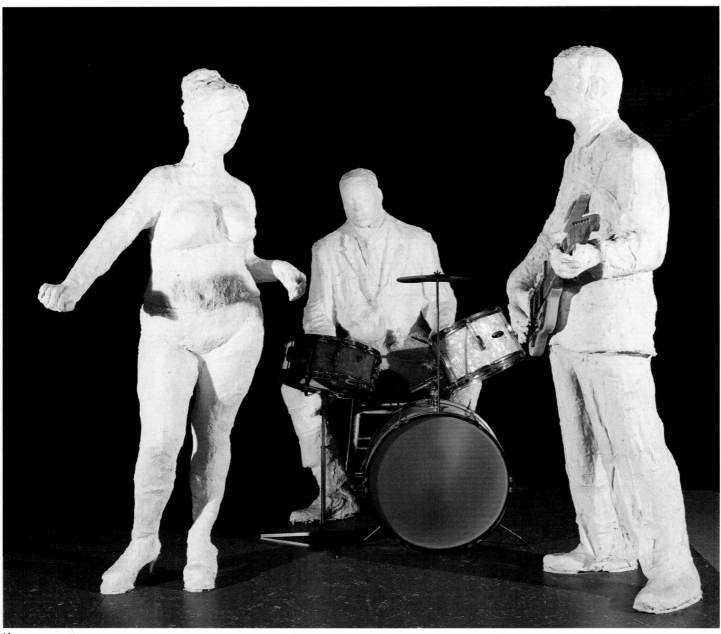

13

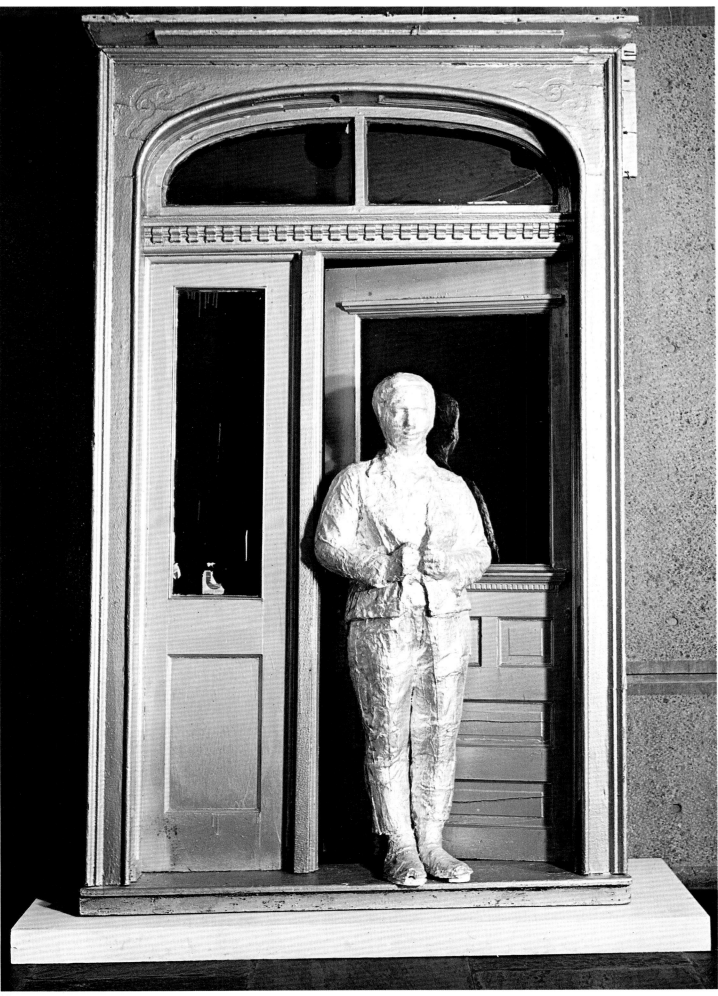

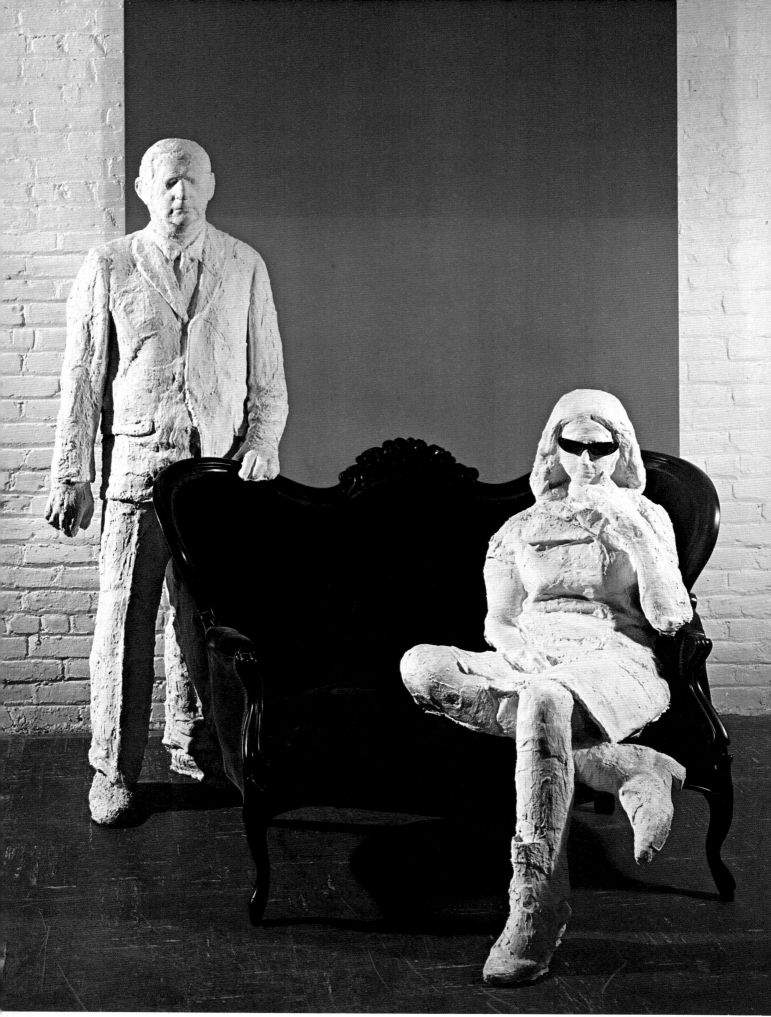

15. *Robert and Ethel Scull*. 1965.
    Plaster, wood, canvas and cloth,
    96×72×72 in (244×183×183 cm).
    Collection of Mr. and Mrs. Robert C. Scull, New York.

16. *The Butcher Shop*. 1965.
    Plaster, metal, wood, vinyl, Plexiglas and other
    objects, 94×99¼×48 in. (239×252×122 cm).
    Art Gallery of Ontario, Toronto
    (Gift from the Women's Committee Fund, 1966).

17. *The Diner*. 1964-1966.
    Plaster, wood, metal Formica,
    Masonite and fluorescent light,
    102×108×87 in. (259×274×221 cm).
    Walker Art Center, Minneapolis, Minnesota.

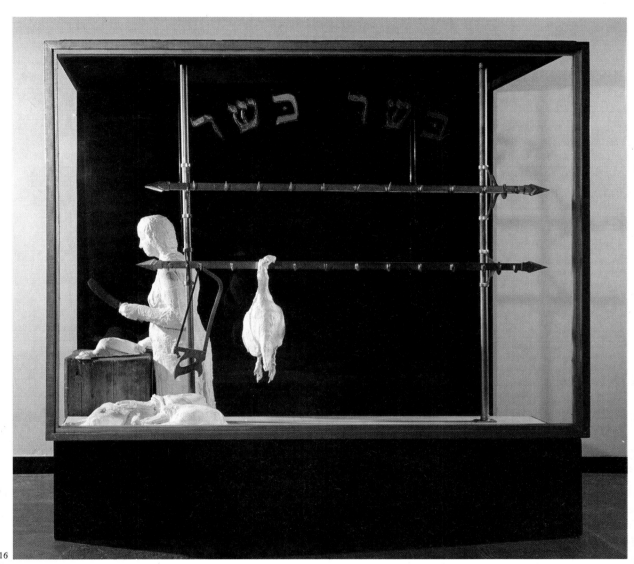

16

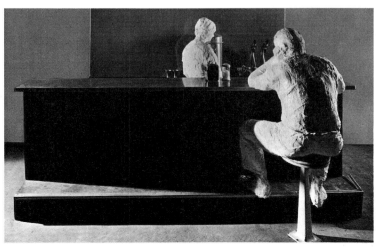

17

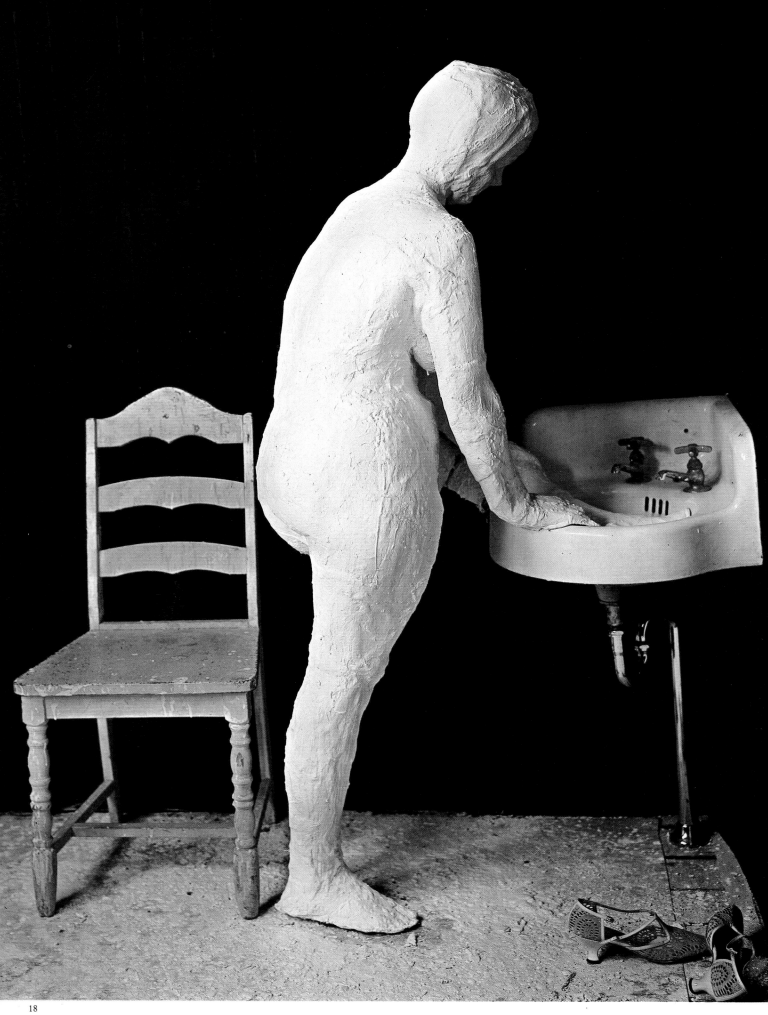

18. *Woman Washing Her Foot in a Sink*. 1965.
    Plaster, wood, metal and porcelain,
    60 × 48 × 36 in. (152.5 × 122 × 91.5 cm).
    Wallraf-Richartz-Museum, Cologne (Ludwig Collection).

19. *The Billboard*. 1966.
    Plaster, wood, metal and rope,
    189 × 117 × 20 in. (480 × 297 × 51 cm).
    South Mall Project, Albany.

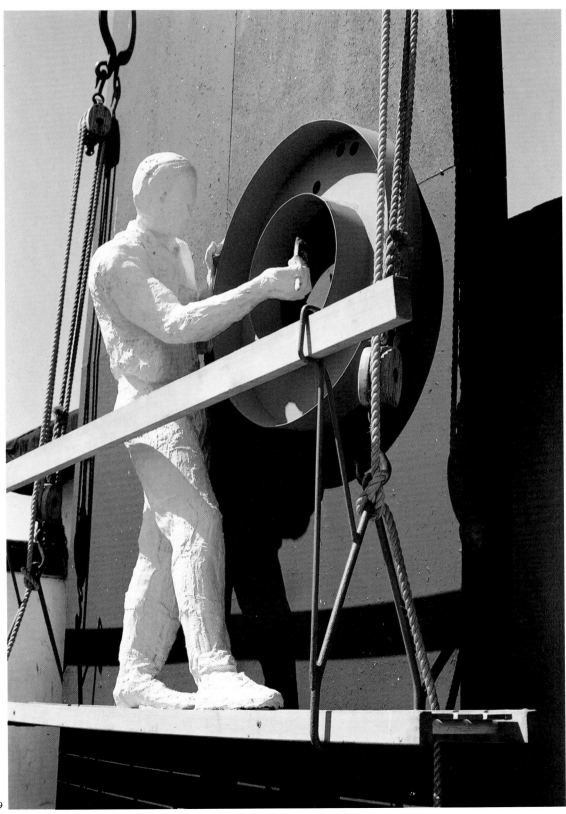

20. *John Chamberlain Working*. 1965-1967.
    Plaster, metal, plastic and aluminum paint,
    69 × 66 × 56 in (175 × 168 × 142 cm).
    The Museum of Modern Art, New York
    (Promised gift of Carroll Janis and Conrad Janis).

21. *Walking Man*. 1966.
    Plaster, wood and painted metal,
    84 × 58 × 34 in. (214 × 147 × 86 cm).
    Collection of Mrs. Norman B. Champ, Jr., Saint Louis.

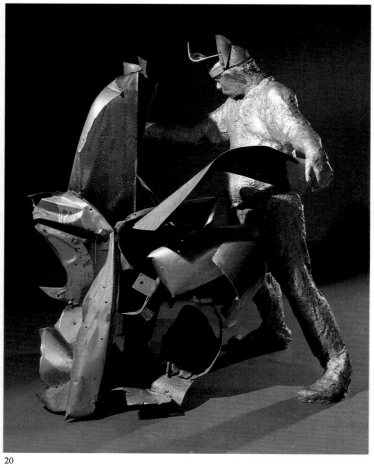

20

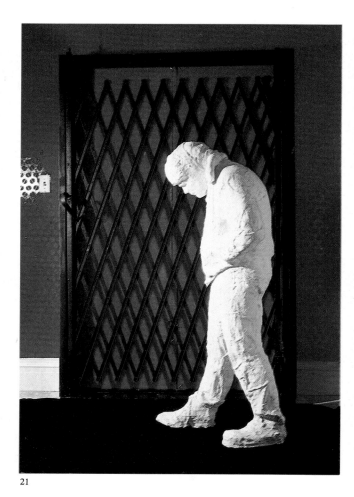

21

22. *The Truck*. 1966.
   Plaster, wood, metal, glass, vinyl and film projector,
   66×60×53 in. (168×152×135 cm).
   Art Institute of Chicago (Mr. and Mrs. Frank G. Logan Fund).

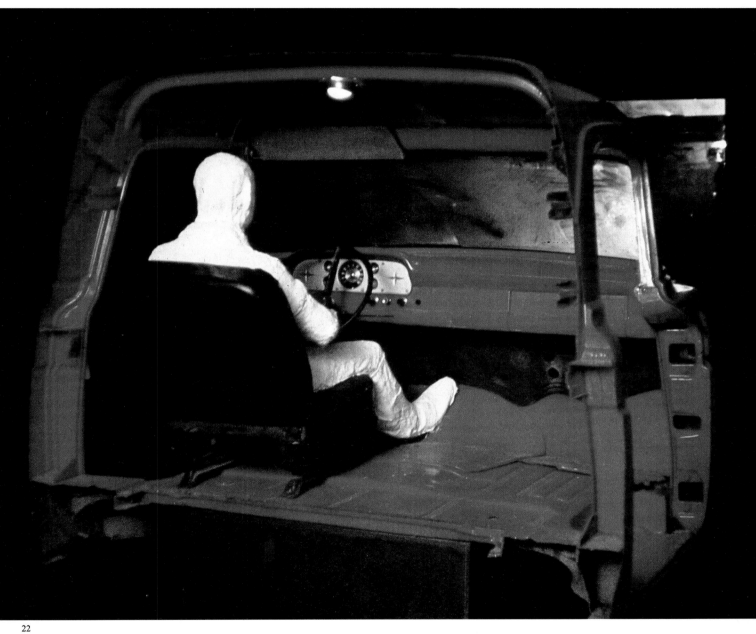

22

23. *The Execution*. 1967.
  Plaster, wood, metal and rope, 96 × 132 × 96 in. (244 × 335 × 244 cm).
  Vancouver Art Gallery.

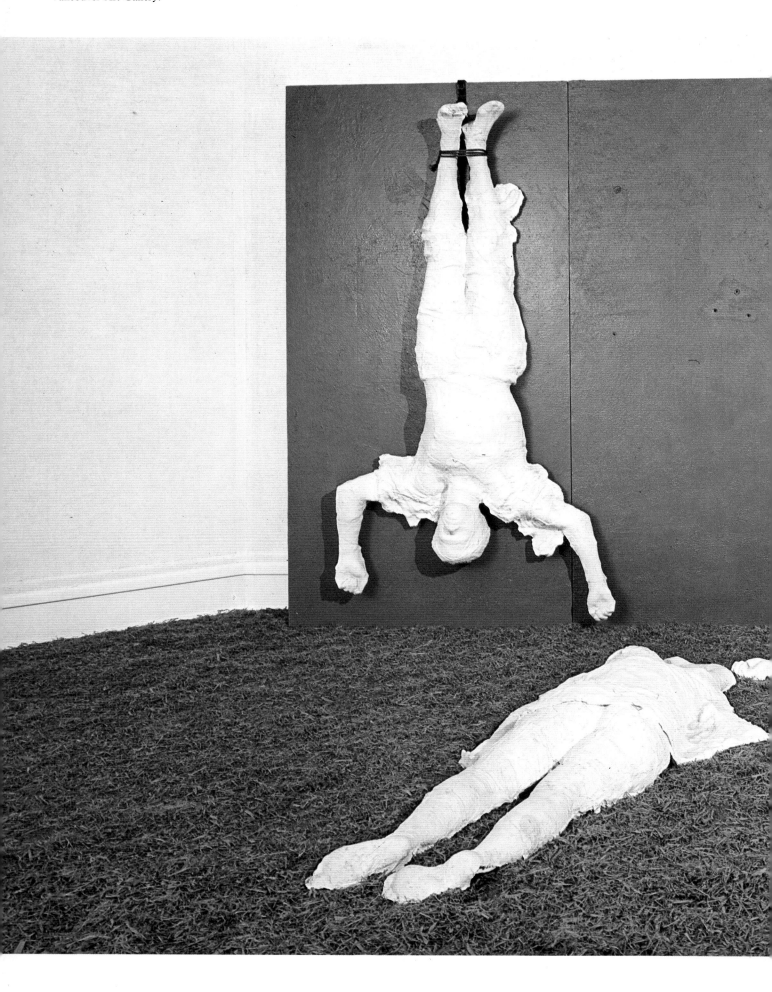

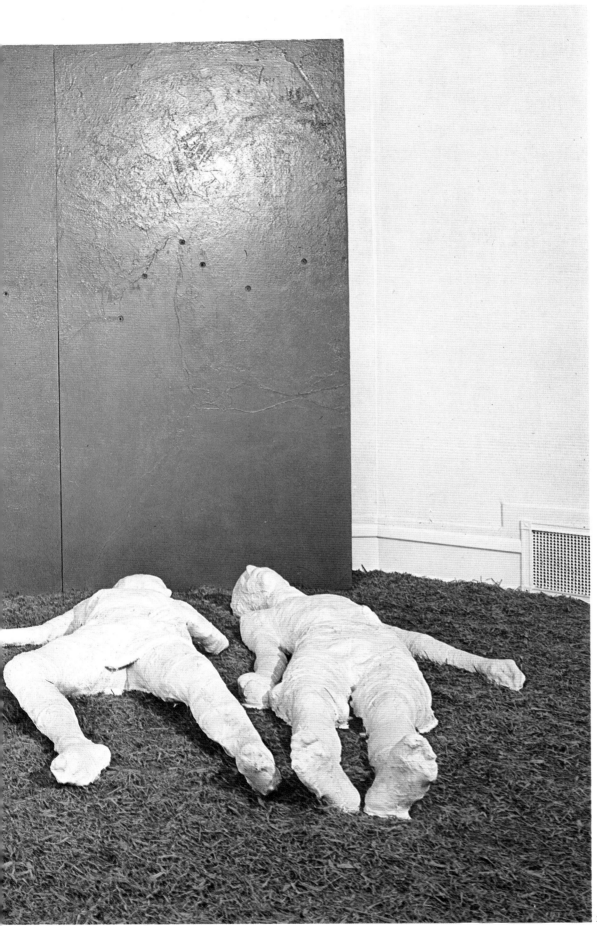

24. *The Parking Garage*. 1968.
Plaster, wood, metal, electrical parts and light bulbs,
120 × 152 × 48 in. (305 × 386 × 122 cm).
Newark Museum, New Jersey.

25. *Man Leaving a Bus*. 1967.
Plaster, painted metal, glass, chrome and rubber,
88½ × 39 × 33½ in. (225 × 99 × 85 cm).
Harry N. Abrams Family Collection, New York

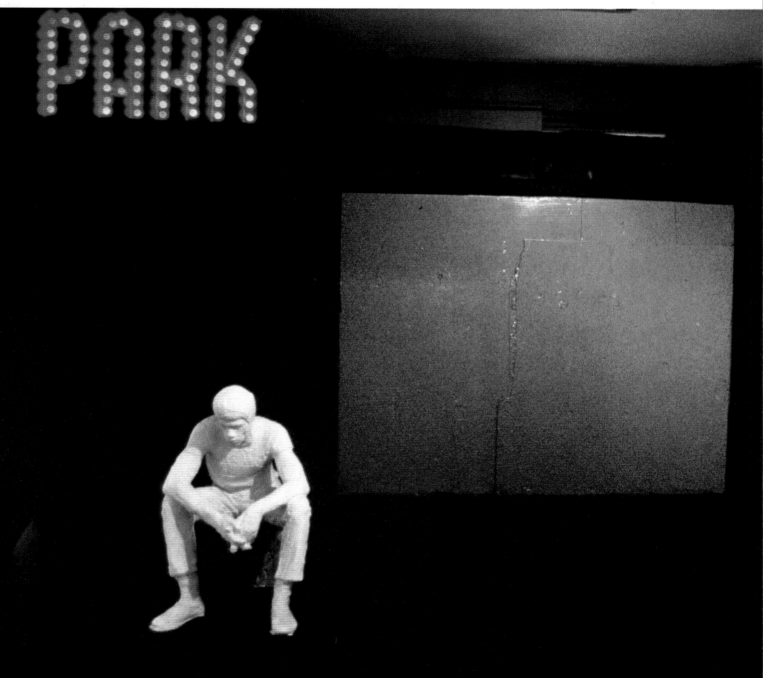

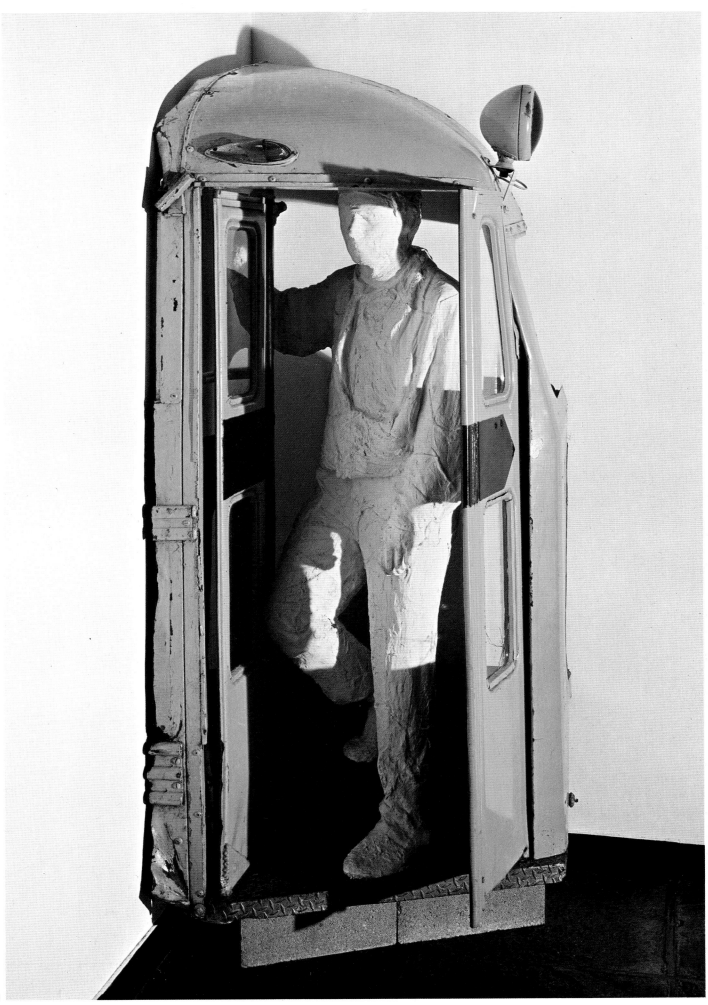

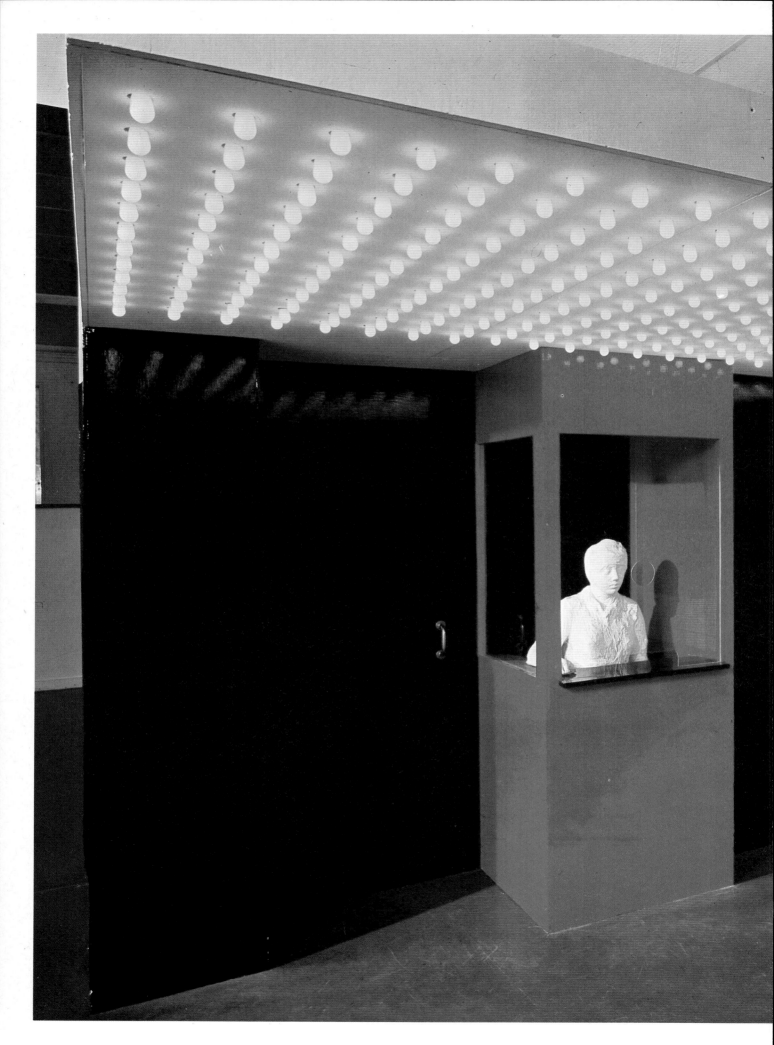

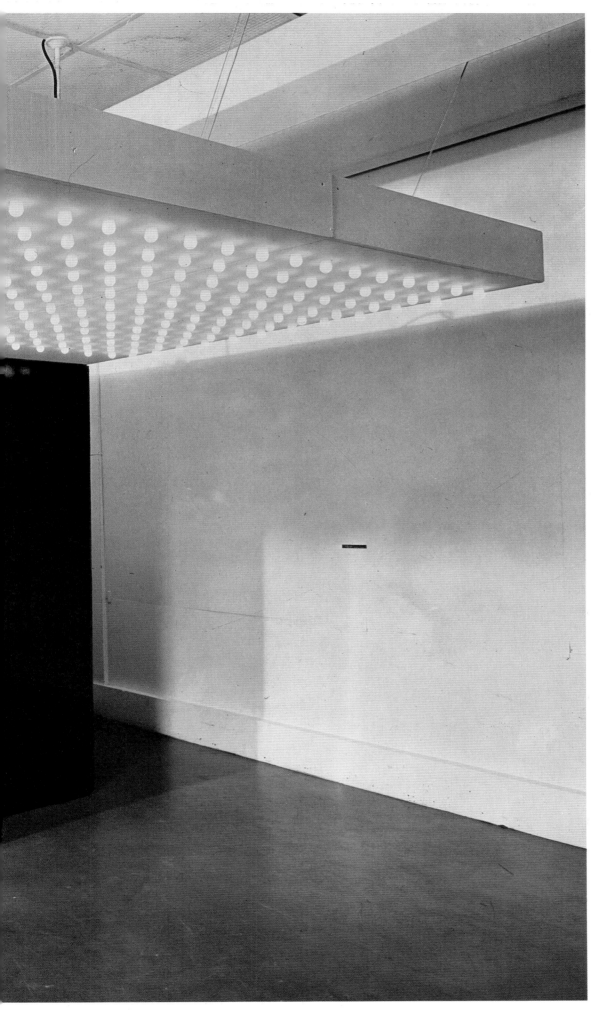

26. *The Moviehouse.*
1966-1967.
Plaster, wood,
plastic and
incandescent lights,
102 × 148 × 153 in.
(259 × 376 × 388 cm).
Musée National
d'Art Moderne,
Paris (on loan
from Centre
National d'Art
Contemporain,
Paris).

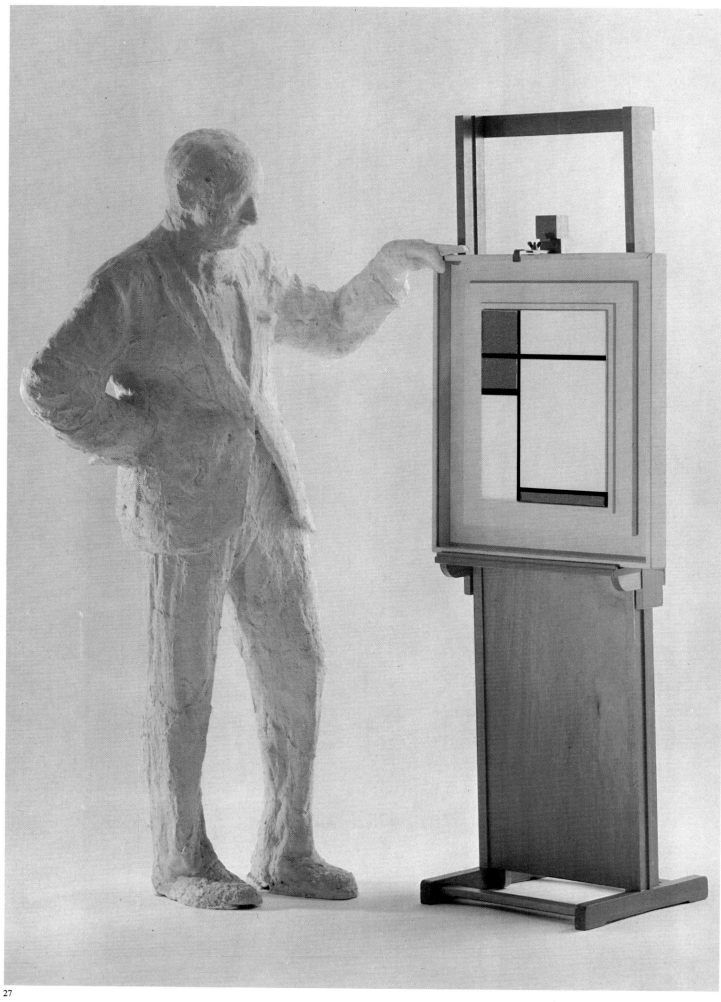

27

27. *Sidney Janis with Mondrian's "Composition" of 1933, on an Easel.* 1967.
    Plaster, wood, metal and canvas,
    67 × 50 × 33 in. (170 × 127 × 84 cm).
    The Museum of Modern Art, New York
    (Sidney and Harriet Janis Collection).

28. *Artist in His Studio.* 1968.
    Plaster, wood, paper and pastel,
    96 × 120 × 108 in. (244 × 305 × 274 cm).
    Collection of Reinhard Onnasch, Berlin.

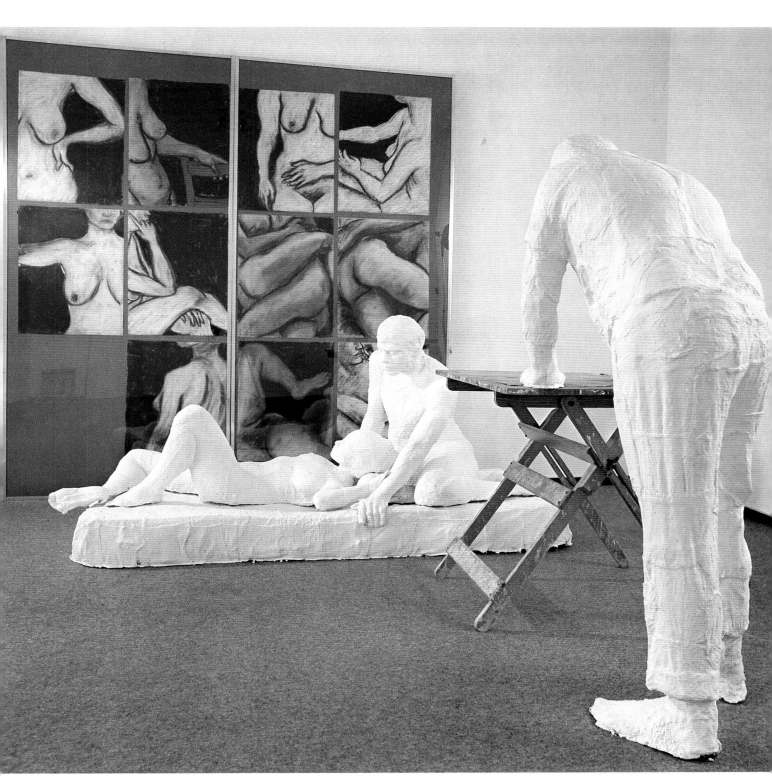

29. *Girl Sitting Against a Wall I*. 1968.
Plaster, wood and glass,
84 × 96 × 37 in. (213 × 244 × 94 cm).
Staatsgalerie Stuttgart, Stuttgart.

30. *The Subway*. 1968.
Plaster, metal, glass, rattan, incandescent light and
electrical parts, 90 × 115 × 53 in. (229 × 292 × 135 cm).
Collection of Mrs. Robert B. Mayer, Chicago.

31. *Construction Tunnel*. 1968.
Plaster, wood and metal,
168 × 60 × 93 in. (427 × 153 × 236 cm).
The Detroit Institute of Arts (Founders Society Purchase).

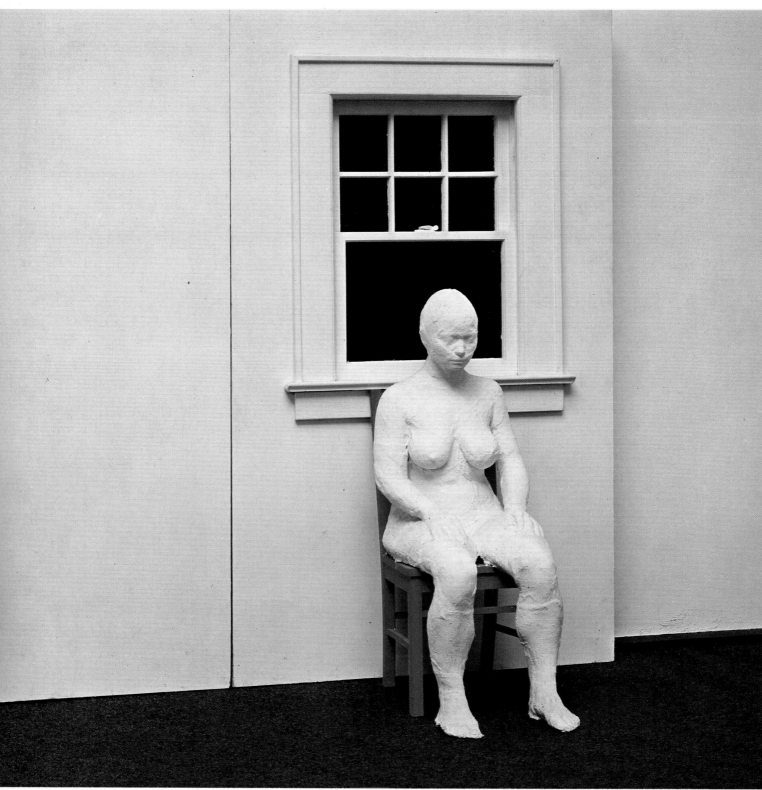

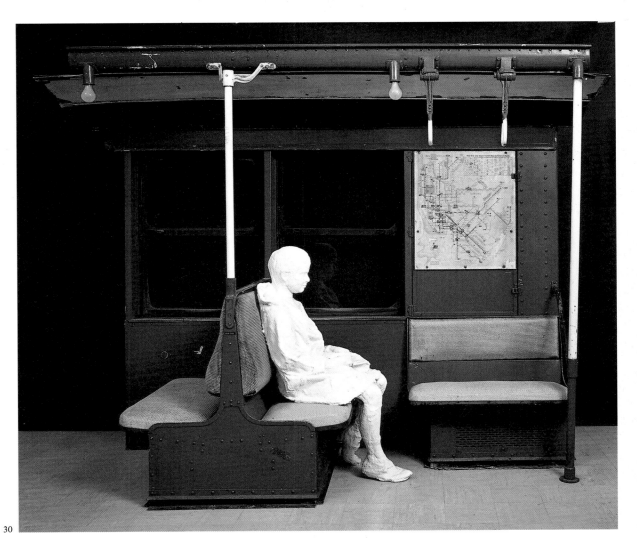

30

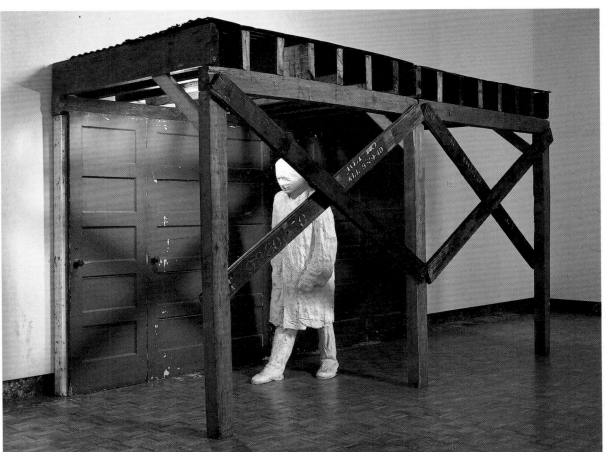

31

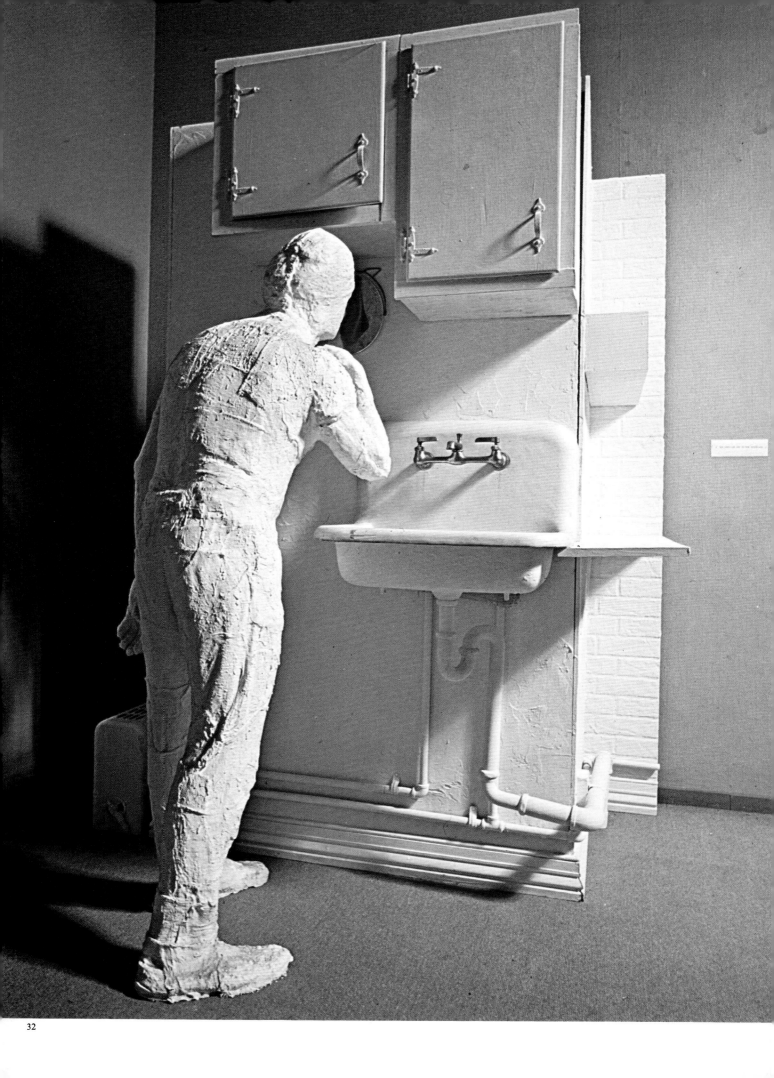

32. *The Artist in His Loft*. 1969.
    Plaster, wood, metal, glass and porcelain,
    90 × 69 × 60 in. (229 × 175 × 152 cm).
    Collection of Reinhard Onnasch, Berlin.

33. *Self-Portrait with Head and Body*. 1968.
    Plaster and wood,
    66 × 32 × 42 in. (168 × 81 × 107 cm).
    Collection of Carter Burden, New York.

34. *Box: Man in a Bar*. 1969.
    Plaster, wood, metal and cloth,
    60 × 24 × 12 in. (152 × 70 × 30 cm).
    Collection of Mr. and Mrs. E. A. Bergman, Chicago.

35. *Box: Woman Looking Through Window*. 1969.
    Plaster, wood, and celotex,
    60 × 24 × 12 in. (152 × 70 × 30 cm).
    Collection of Serge de Bloe, Brussels.

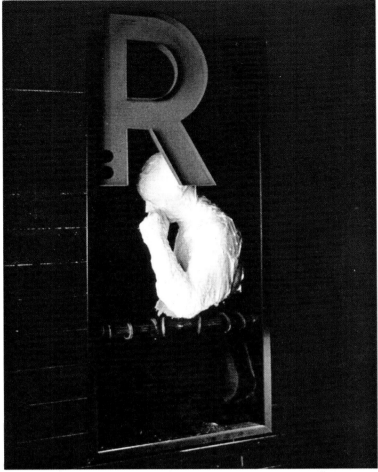

34

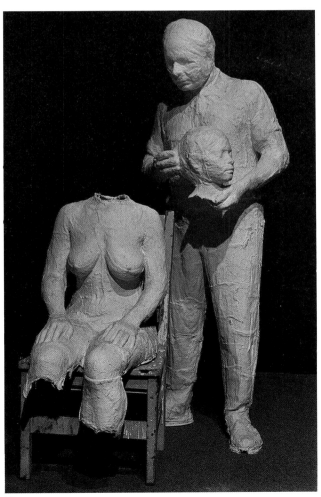

33

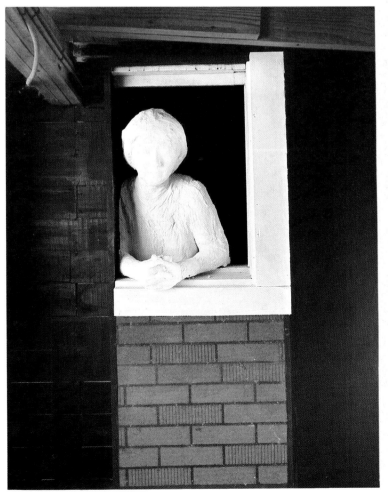

35

36. *The Brick Wall*. 1970.
   Plaster, wood and plastic,
   96 × 152 × 42 in. (244 × 386 × 107 cm).
   Gatodo Gallery, Tokyo, Japan.

37. *Lovers on a Bed II*. 1970.
   Plaster and metal,
   48 × 72 × 60 in. (122 × 183 × 152 cm).
   Phillip Johnson Collection, New York.

38. *Girl Walking Out of the Ocean*. 1970.
   Plaster and wood,
   84 × 60 × 28½ in. (213 × 152 × 72 cm).
   Private collection, Brussels.

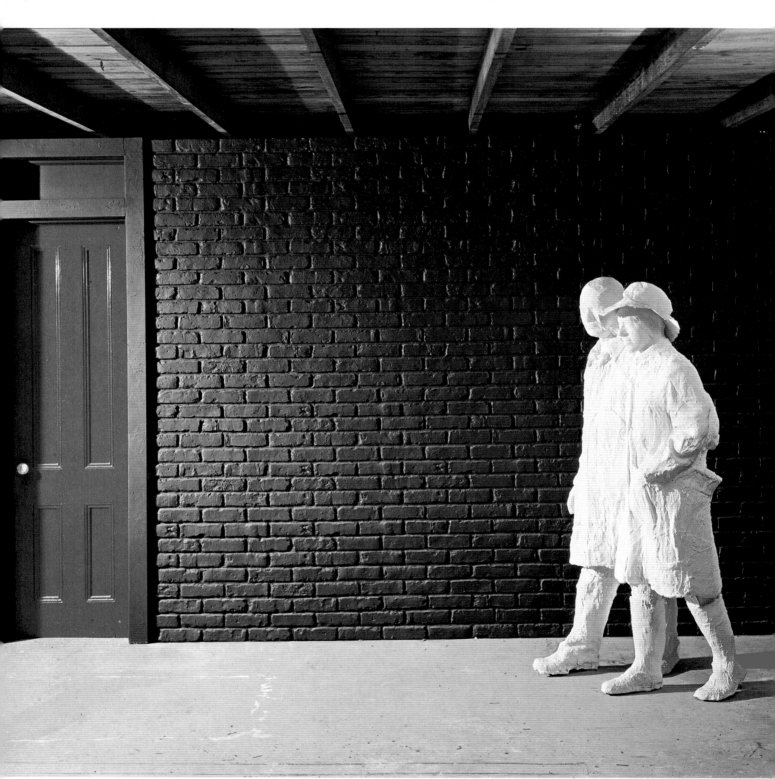

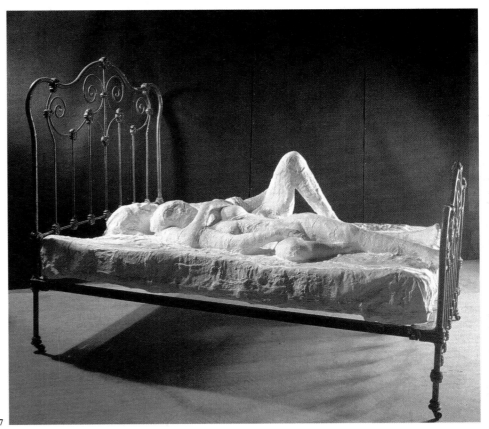

37

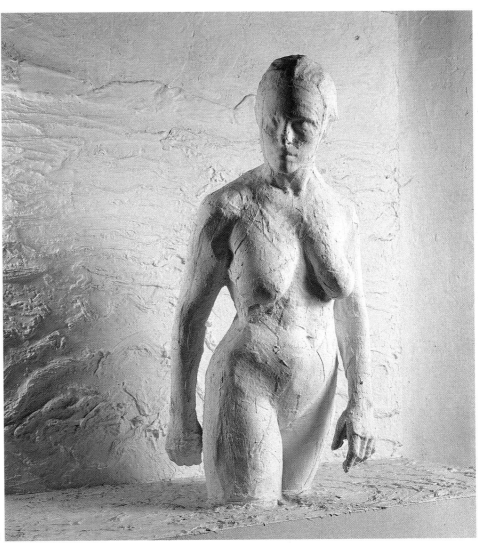

38

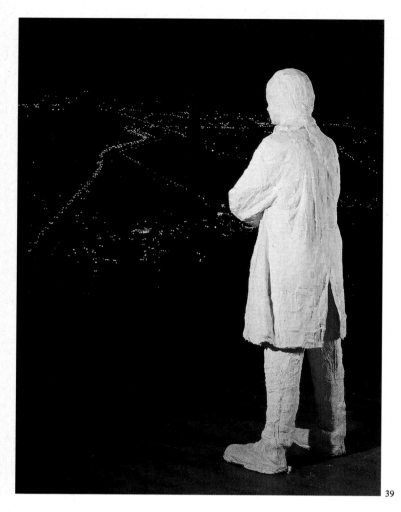

39

39. *The Aerial View*. 1970.
Plaster, wood, plastic, incandescent and fluorescent light, 96 × 105 × 48 in. (244 × 267 × 121 cm).
The Art Museum of the Atenaeum, Helsinki (Collection Sara Hilden).

40. *Alice Listening to Her Poetry and Music*. 1970.
Plaster, wood, glass and tape recorder, 96 × 96 × 33 in. (244 × 244 × 84 cm).
Staatsgalerie Moderner Kunst, Munich.

41. *Times Square at Night*. 1970.
Plaster, wood, plastic, incandescent and fluorescent light, 108 × 96 × 60 in. (274 × 244 × 152 cm).
Joslyn Art Museum, Omaha, Nebraska.

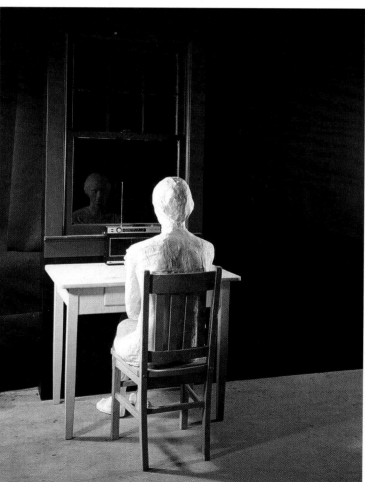

40

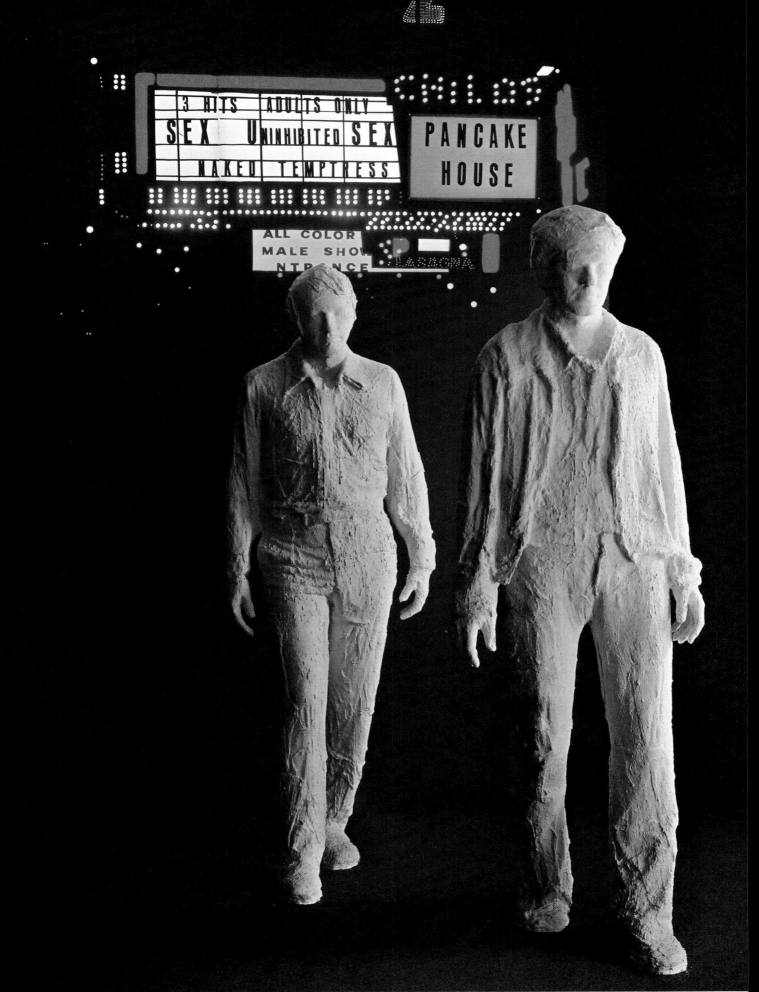

42. *The Bowery*. 1970.
Plaster, wood and metal,
96×96×72 in. (244×244×183 cm).
Kunsthaus, Zurich.

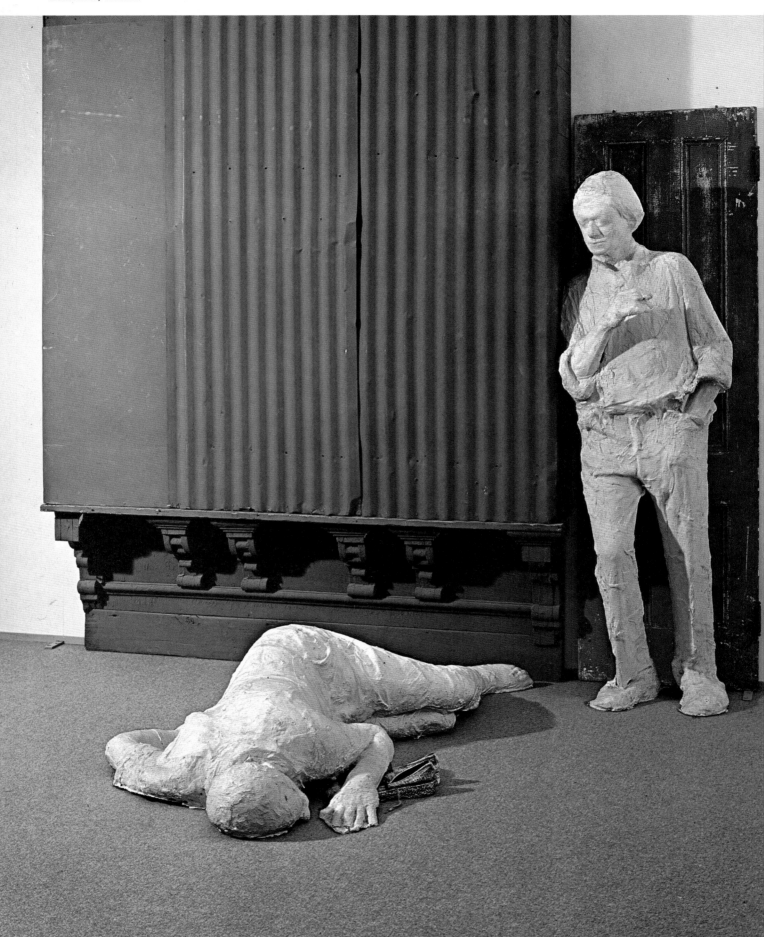

43-44. *The Bar*. 1971.
Plaster, wood, metal, glass, plastic, neon light
and television, 96 × 102 × 36 in. (243 × 259 × 91.5 cm).
Collection of Martin Z. Margulies, Grove Isle, Florida.

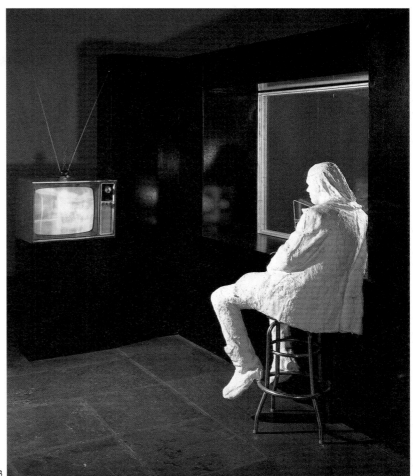

43

44

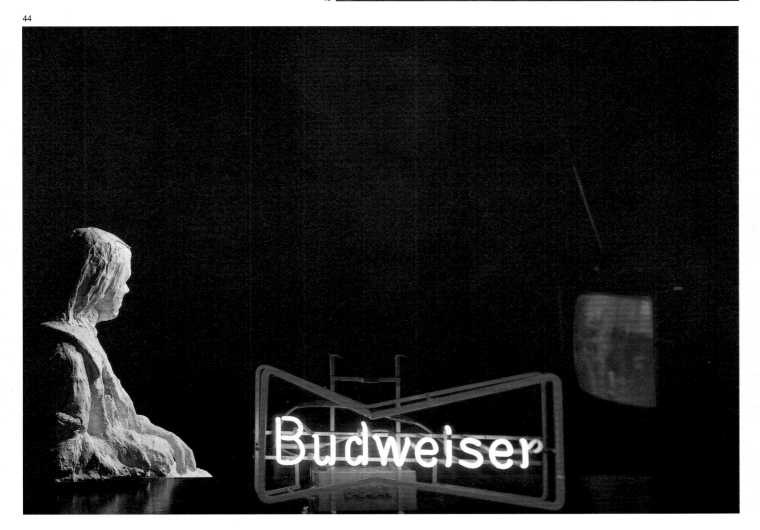

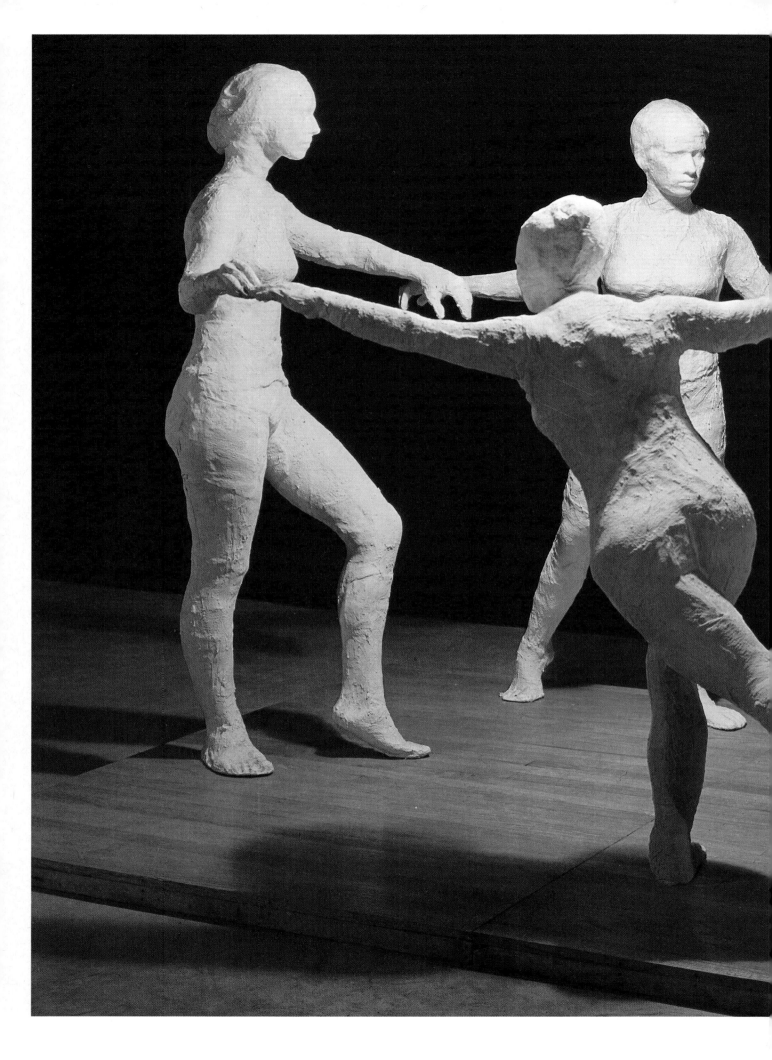

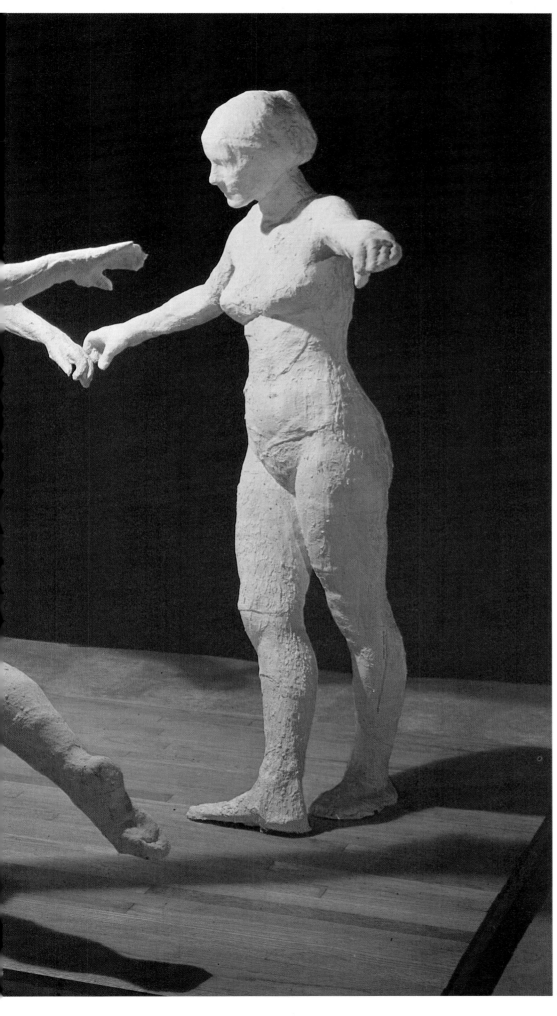

45. *The Dancers*. 1971.
   Bronze,
   72 × 144 × 96 in.
   (183 × 366 × 244 cm).
   National Gallery of Art,
   Washington, D.C. (2/5).

46. *To All Gates*. 1971.
    Plaster, wood, metal, plastic and fluorescent light,
    96 × 144 × 96 in. (244 × 366 × 244 cm).
    Des Moines Art Center (Coffin Fine Arts Trust Fund).

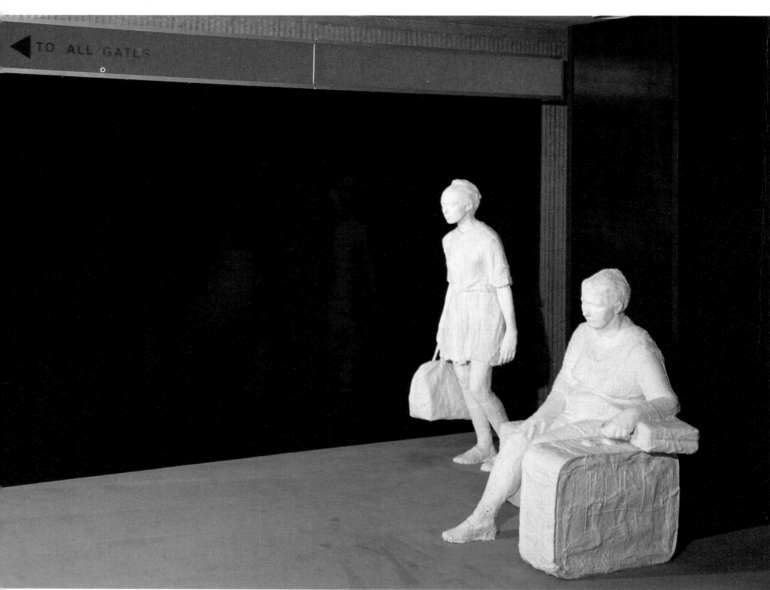

46

47. *Man Standing on a Printing Press*. 1971.
Plaster, wood and metal,
96 × 96 × 24 in. (244 × 244 × 70 cm).
Des Moines Register & Tribune Company,
Des Moines, Iowa.

48. *Girl Looking Through Window*. 1972.
Plaster and mixed media,
96 × 36 × 24 in. (244 × 91 × 70 cm).
Museum Boymans-van Beuningen, Rotterdam.

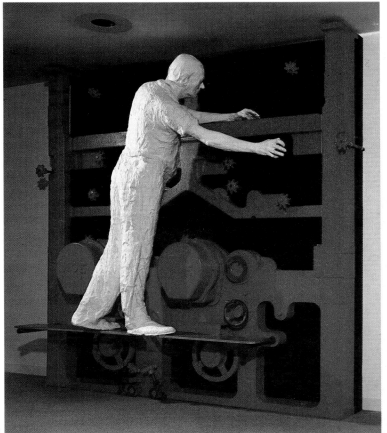

47

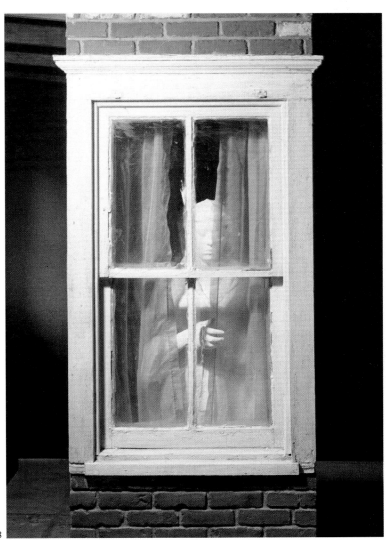

48

49. *The Costume Party* (Final Version). 1965-1972.
    Acrylic on plaster, metal, wood and mixed media,
    72 × 144 × 108 in. (183 × 366 × 274 cm).
    Courtesy of Sidney Janis Gallery, New York.

50. *The Red Light*. 1972.
    Plaster and mixed media,
    114 × 96 × 36 in. (290 × 244 × 91 cm).
    Cleveland Museum of Art (Andrew R. and Martha Holden Jennings Fund).

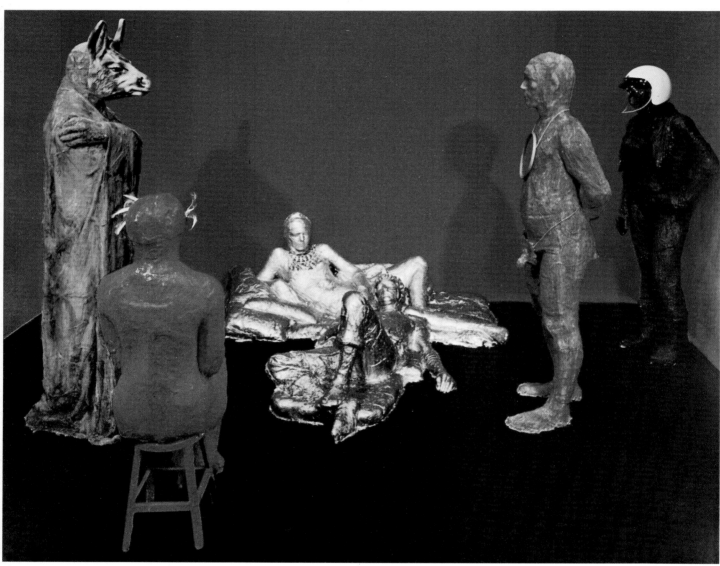

49

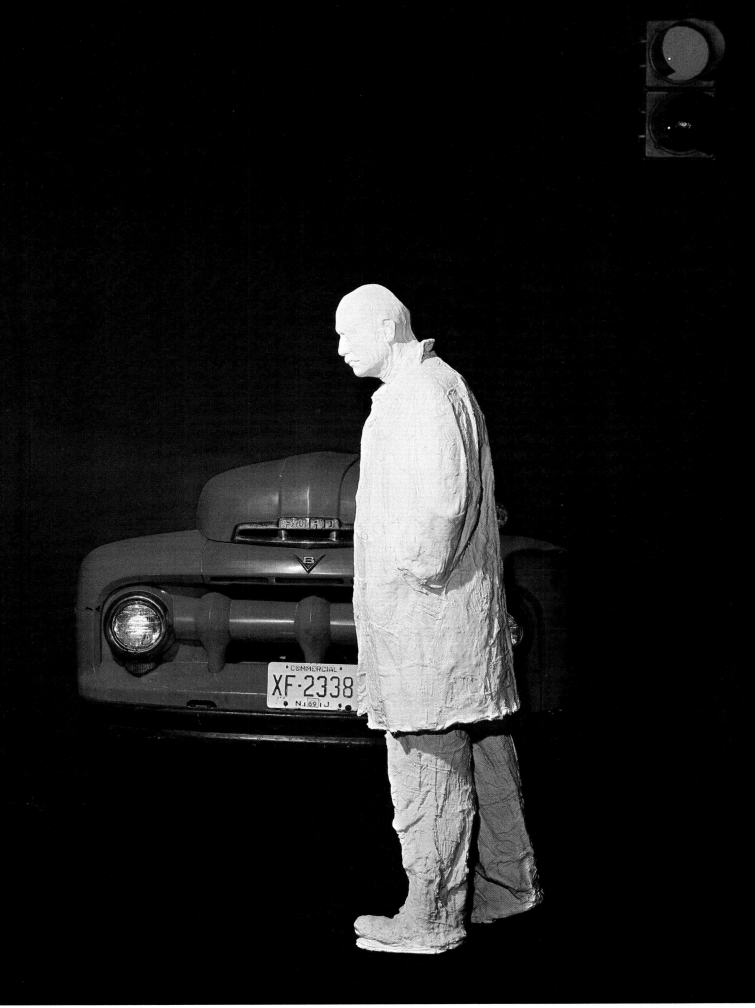

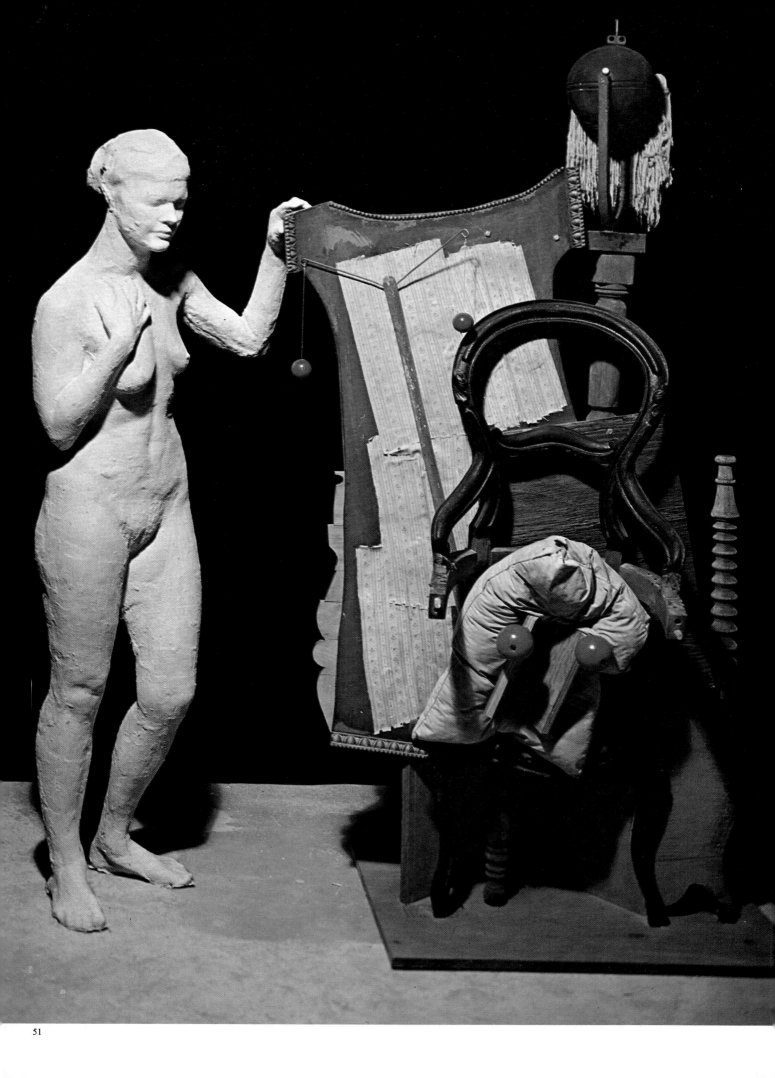

51. *Picasso's Chair*. 1973.
    Plaster and mixed media,
    78×60 in. (198×152 cm).
    Guggenheim Museum, New York.

52. *Girl on Blanket: Hand on Leg*. 1973.
    Plaster, 50×39×10 in. (127×99×25 cm).
    Collection of Mr. and Mrs. Robert Kardon,
    Philadelphia, Pennsylvania.

53. *Girl on Red Wicker Couch*. 1973.
    Plaster and mixed media,
    35×80×58 in. (89×203×147 cm).
    Hopkins Center Art Gallery, Dartmouth College,
    Hanover, New Hampshire.

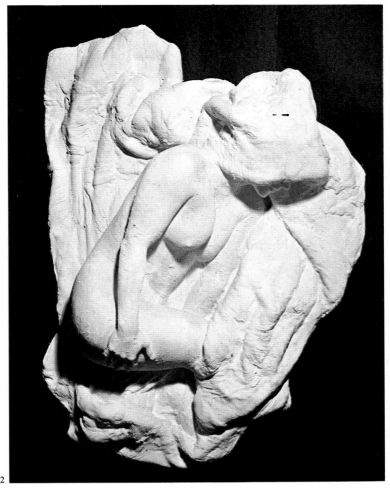

52

53

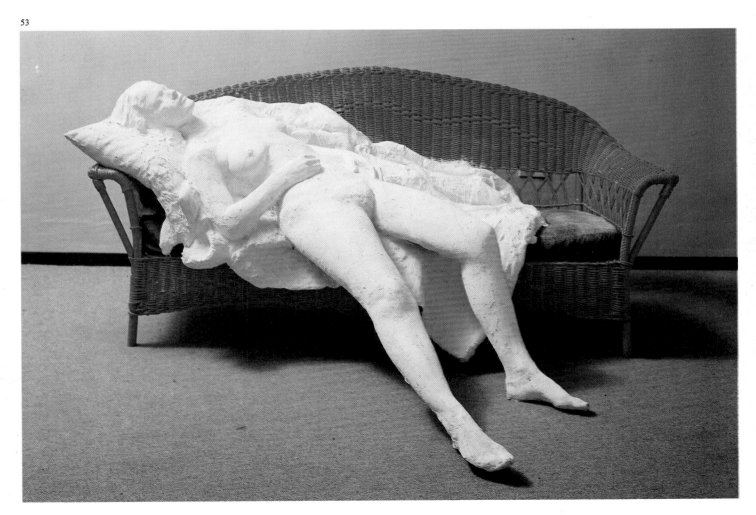

54. *Girl Drying Her Knee.* 1973.
    Plaster, aluminum and cloth,
    59×24×44 in. (150×70×112 cm).
    Collection of Ercole Lauro, Naples.

55. *Waitress Pouring Coffee.* 1973.
    Plaster, wood, metal and porcelain,
    96×42×34 in (244×107×86 cm).
    Shiga Museum of Art, Otsu, Japan.

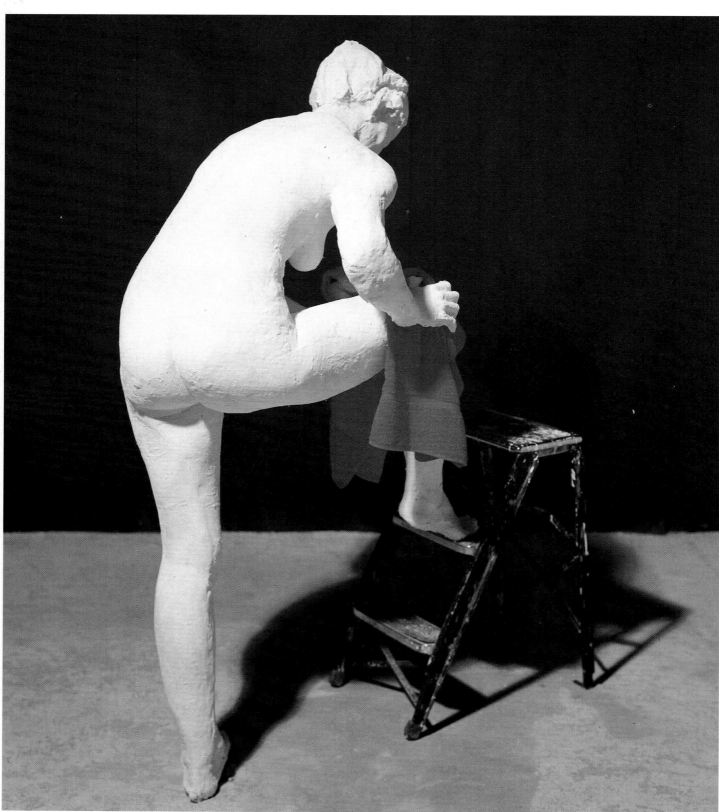

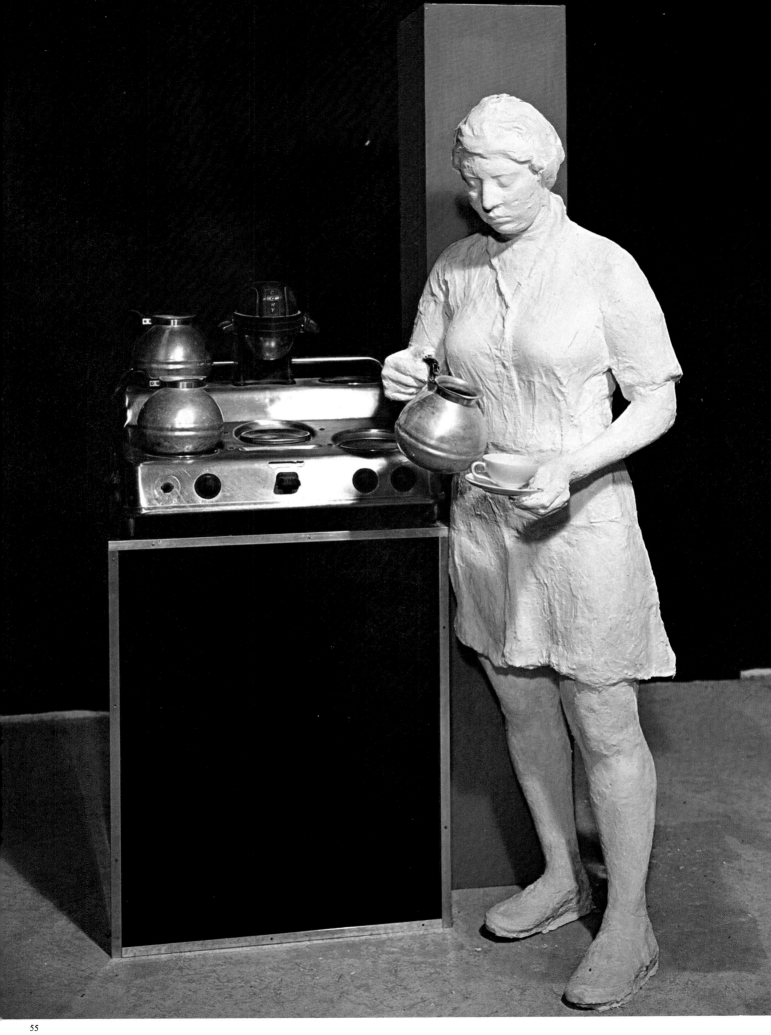

56. *Girl on Red Chair with Blue Robe*. 1974.
Plaster, wood and acrylic,
96½ × 48 × 45 in. (245 × 122 × 114 cm).
Collection of Leonard and Gloria Luria, Miami, Florida.

57. *Girl in Robe I*. 1974.
Plaster, 33 × 14½ × 8 in. (84 × 37 × 20 cm).
Courtesy of Sidney Janis Gallery, New York.

58. *Girl in Robe III*. 1974.
Plaster, 36¼ × 18 × 9 in. (92 × 46 × 23 cm).
Collection of D. Makler Gallery, Philadelphia, Pennsylvania.

59. *Girl Seated on Gray Chair*. 1974.
Plaster, wood and plastic,
36 × 26⅛ × 20¾ in. (91 × 66 × 52 cm).
Courtesy of Sidney Janis Gallery, New York.

60. *The Blue Robe*. 1974.
Plaster and cloth,
49 × 36¾ × 14½ in. (124 × 93 × 37 cm).
Courtesy of Sidney Janis Gallery, New York.

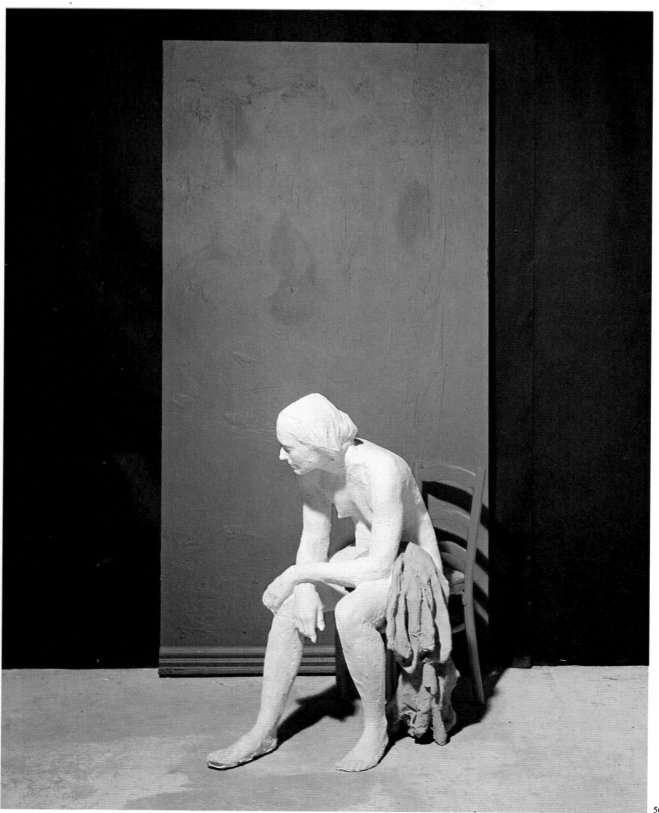

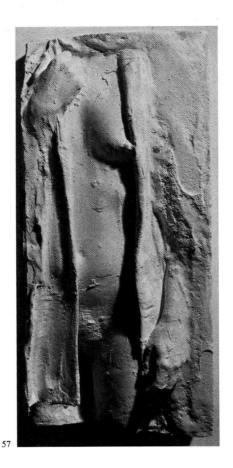

57

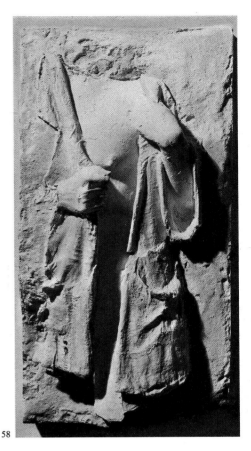

58

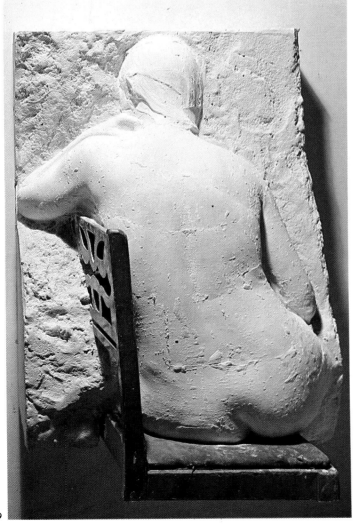

59

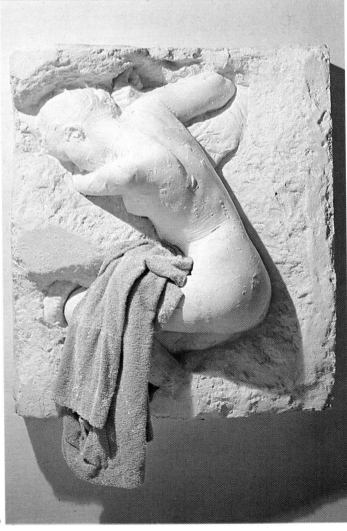

60

61. *Girl Emerging from Tile Wall*. 1974.
Plastic and ceramic tile,
39 × 16⅜ × 10 in. (99 × 42 × 25 cm).
Collection of Barry Boonshaft, Quakertown, Pennsylvania.

62. *Embracing Couple*. 1975.
Plaster, 34 × 30¾ × 11½ in. (86 × 78 × 29 cm).
Martin Friedman, Walker Art Center, Minneapolis, Minnesota.

63. *Two Torsos*. 1975.
Plaster, 41 × 30 × 9 in. (104 × 76 × 23 cm).
Collection of Robert Weiss, Chicago, Illinois.

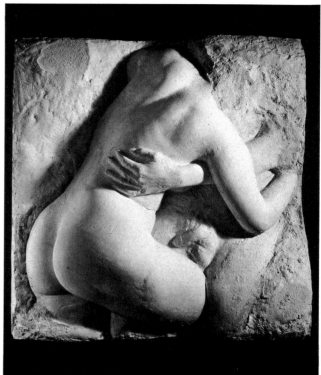

62

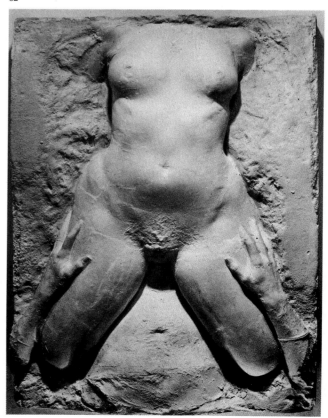

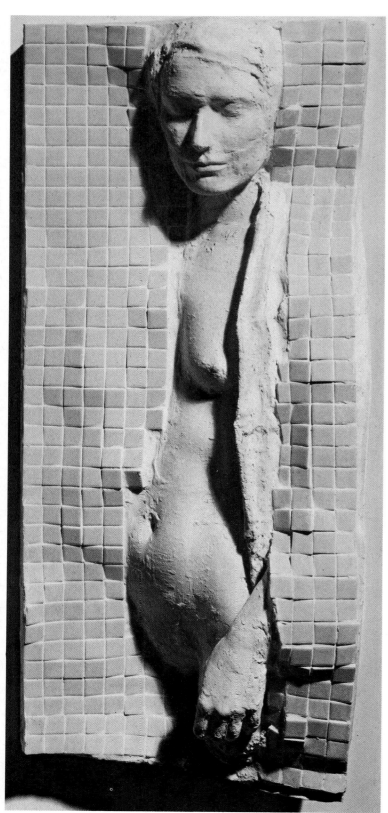

61

63

64. *Girl Next to Chimney* (Version 1). 1975.
Plaster, wood and plastic,
32½ × 40 × 11½ in. (83 × 102 × 29 cm).
Courtesy of Sidney Janis Gallery, New York.

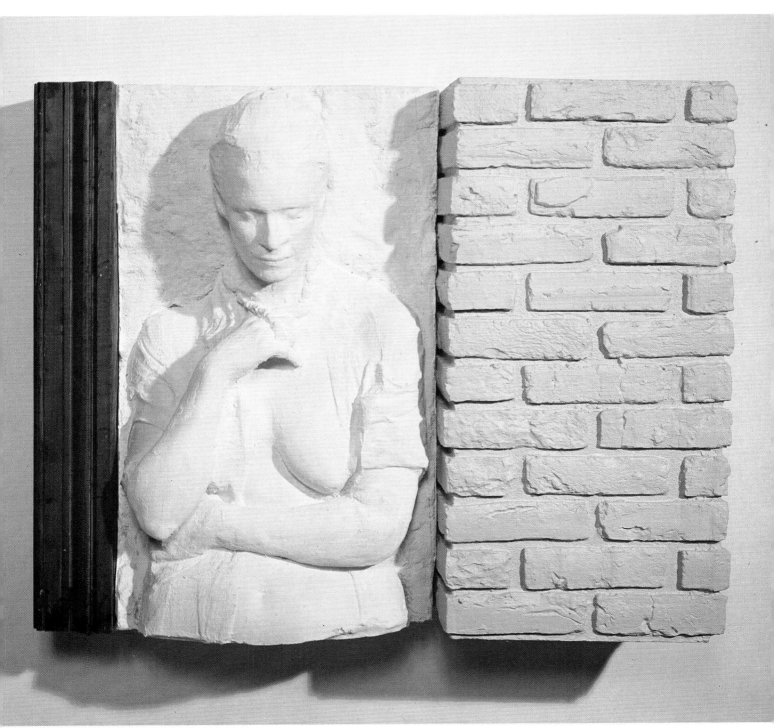

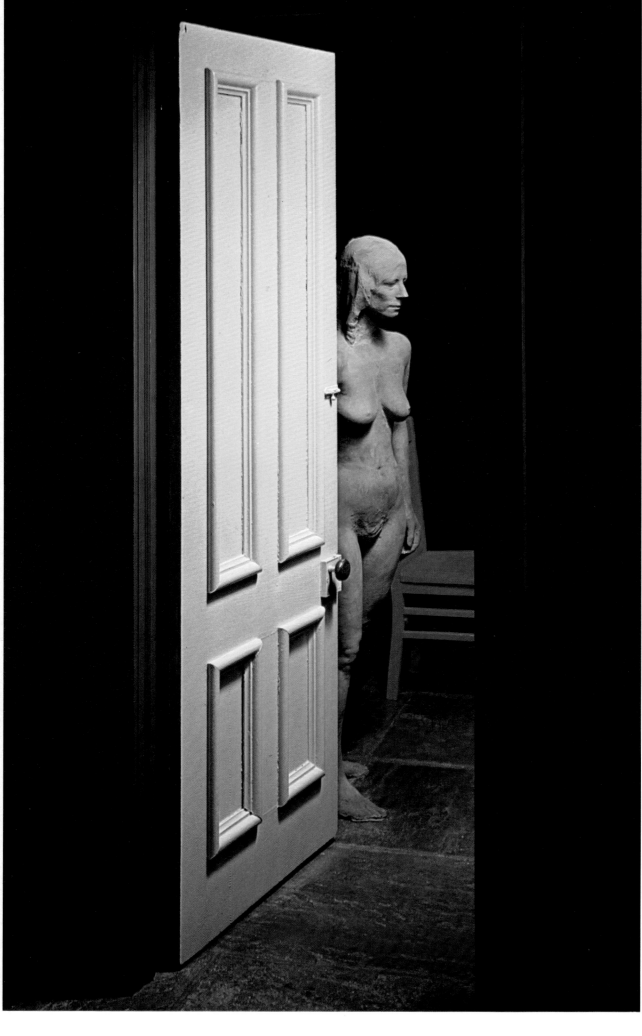

65. *The Corridor*. 1975.
   Plaster and wood,
   84 × 84 × 48 in. (213 × 213 × 122 cm).
   Tamayo Museum, Mexico City, Mexico.

66. *Exit*. 1975.
   Plaster, wood, plastic and electric light,
   84 × 72 × 36 in (213 × 182 × 91.5 cm).
   Philadelphia Museum of Art (Gift of the Friends
   of the Philadelphia of Art Museum).

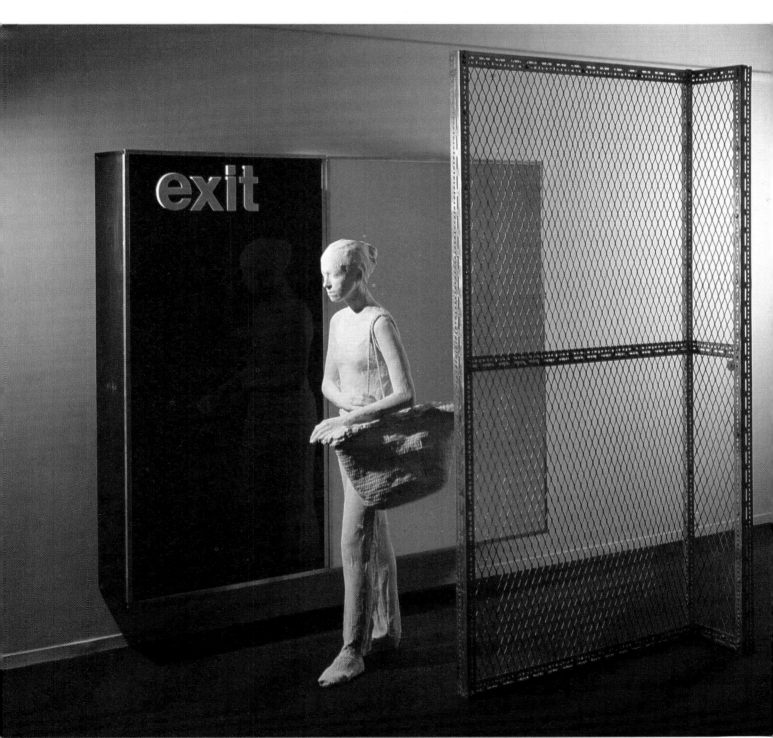

67. *The Restaurant*. 1976.
    Bronze, brick, cement, steel, aluminum, tempered glass,
    and fluorescent light,
    120 × 192 × 96 in. (305 × 488 × 244 cm).
    Federal Office Building, Buffalo.

68. *Girl Standing in Nature*. 1976.
    Bronze, 67 in. high (170 cm).
    Collection of City of Greenwich, Connecticut.

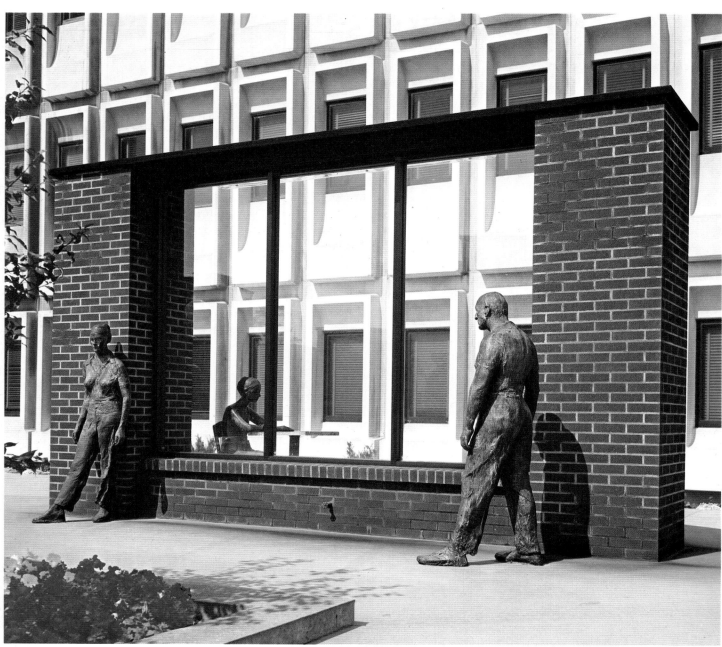

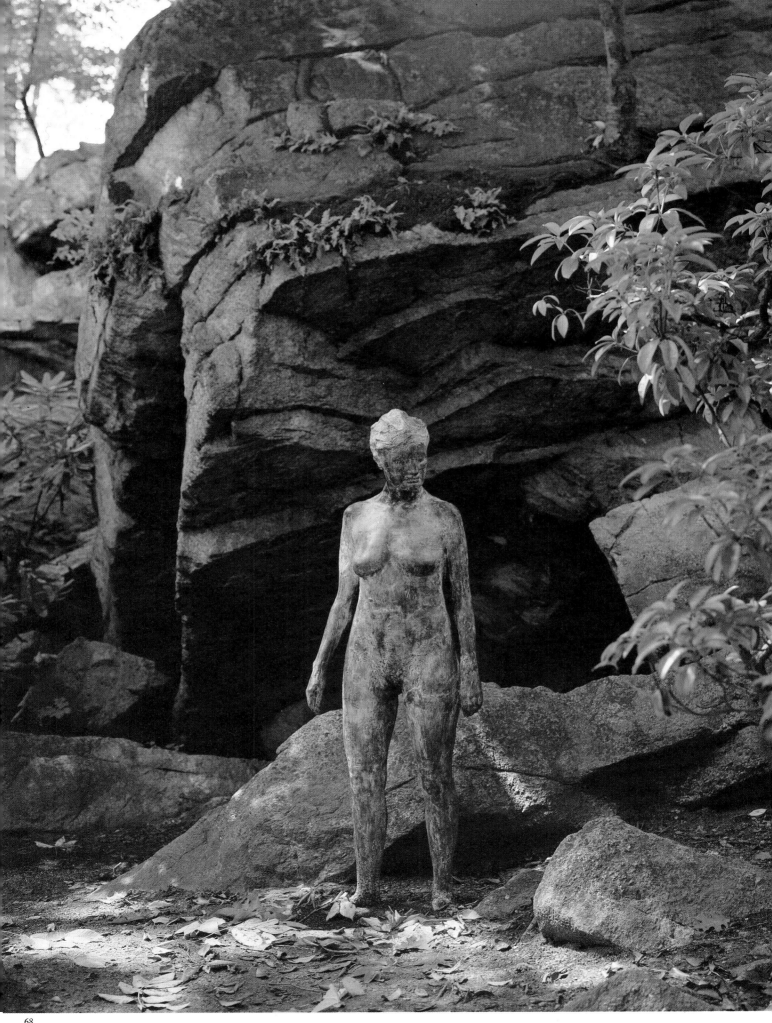

69. *Post No Bills*. 1976.
    Work destroyed.

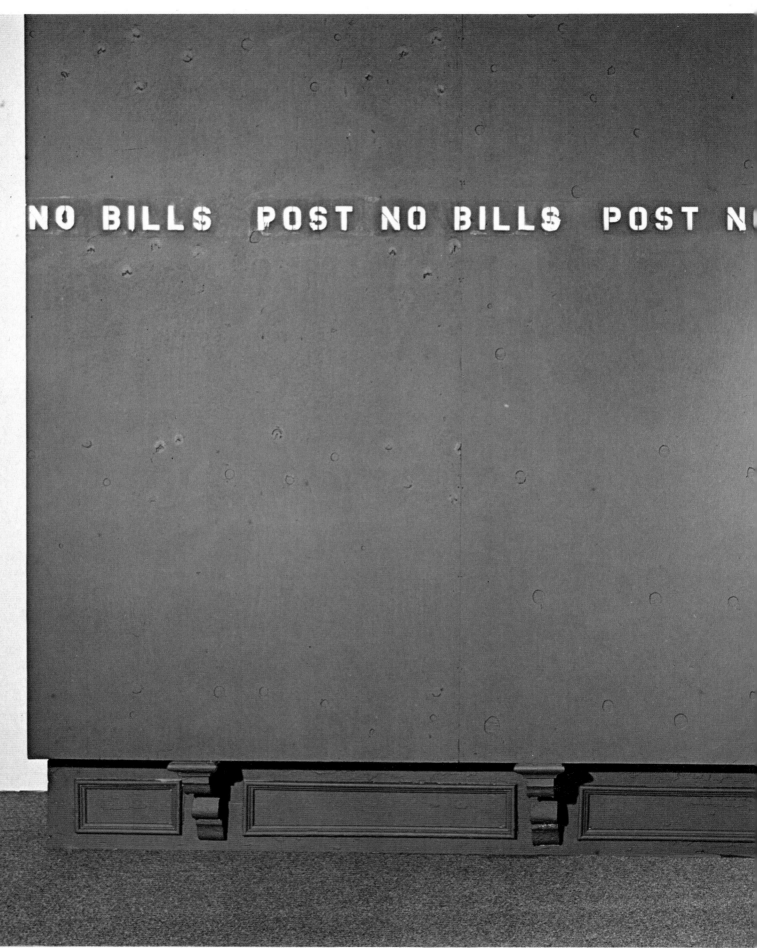

BILLS

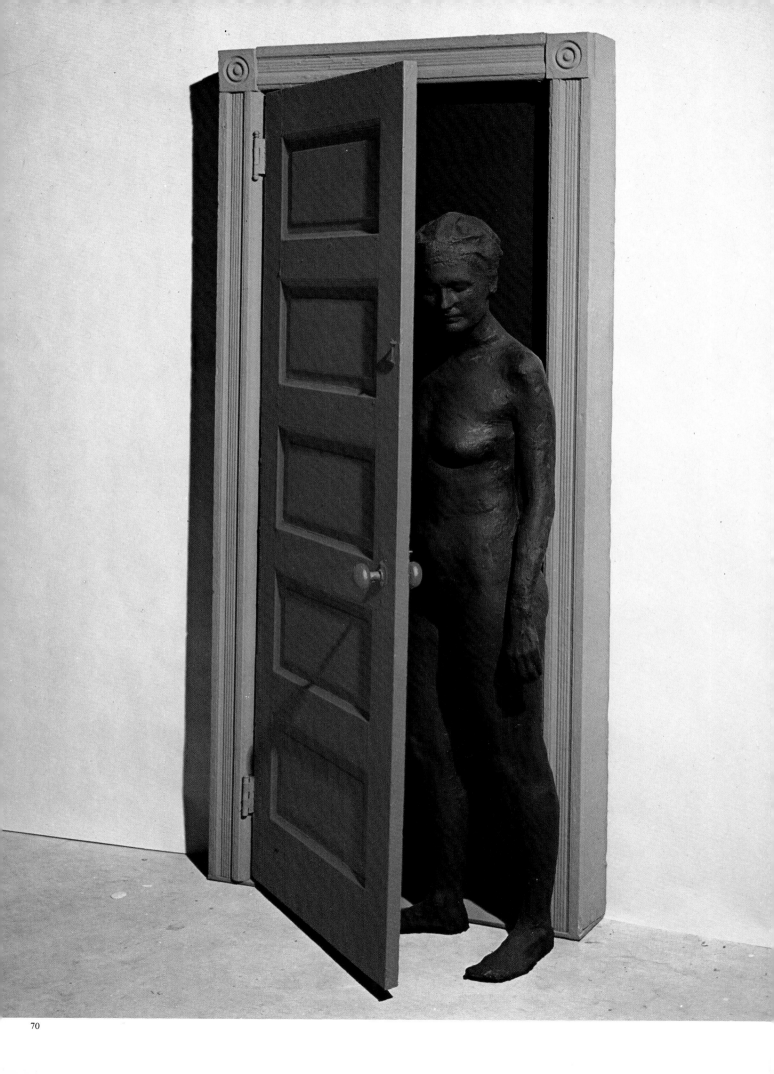

70. *Black Girl Behind Red Door*. 1976.
Painted plaster and wood,
82 × 38 × 24 in. (208 × 97 × 61 cm).
Collection of Madame Landau, Paris.

71. *Walk, Don't Walk*. 1976.
Plaster, cement, metal, painted wood and electric light,
104 × 72 × 72 in. (264 × 183 × 183 cm).
Whitney Museum of American Art, New York.

72. *Red Girl Behind Red Door*. 1976.
Painted plaster and wood,
91 × 50 × 25 in. (231 × 127 × 64 cm).
Collection of Irma and Norman Braman, Miami, Florida.

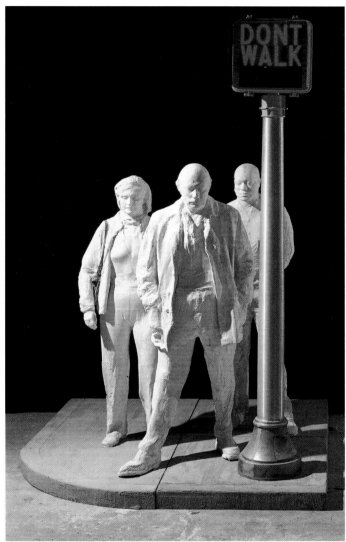

71

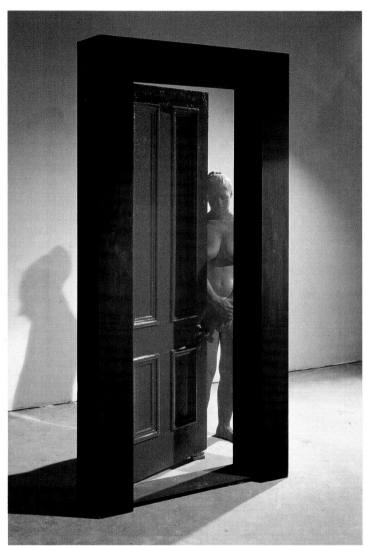

72

73. *Couple on Black Bed*. 1976.
Painted plaster and wood,
44 × 82 × 60 in. (112 × 208 × 152 cm).
Collection of Sydney and Frances Lewis Foundation, Virginia.

74. *Flesh Nude in Blue Field II*. 1977.
Painted plaster and wood,
37¾ × 16½ × 7½ in. (96 × 42 × 19 cm).
Courtesy of Sidney Janis Gallery, New York.

75. *Magenta Girl on Green Door*. 1977.
Painted plaster and painted wood,
72½ × 23 × 12 in. (184 × 58 × 30 cm).
Dr. Milton D. Ratner Family Collection.

76. *Brown Girl*. 1977.
Painted plaster, 35 × 12 × 10½ in. (89 × 30 × 27 cm).
Courtesy of Sidney Janis Gallery, New York.

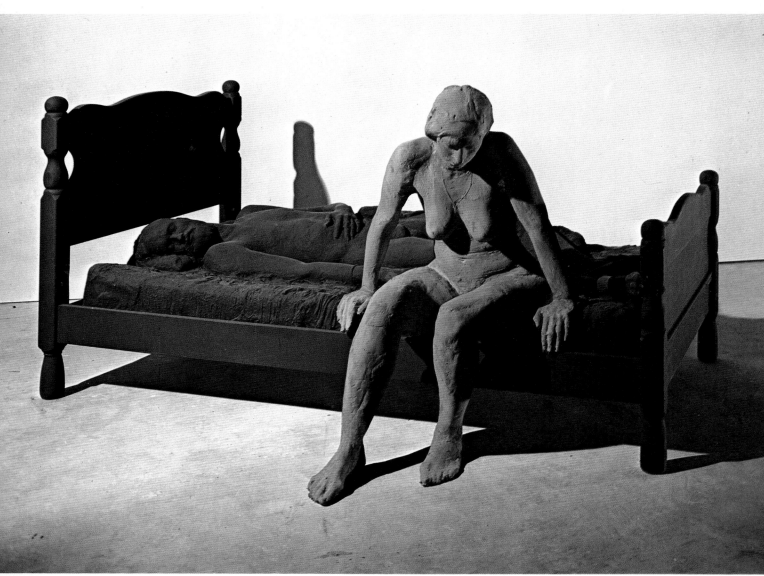

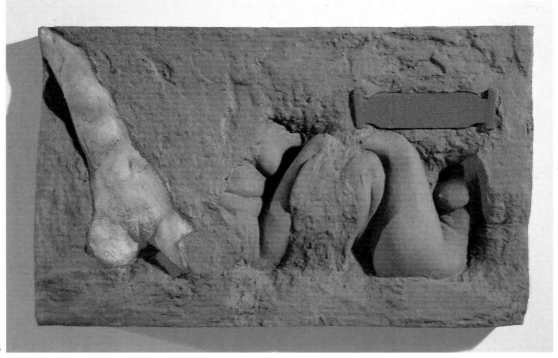

74

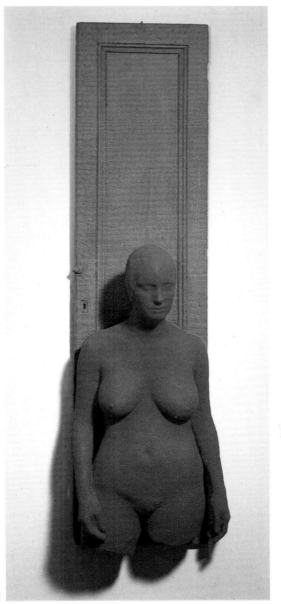

75

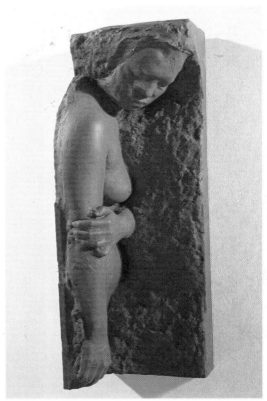

76

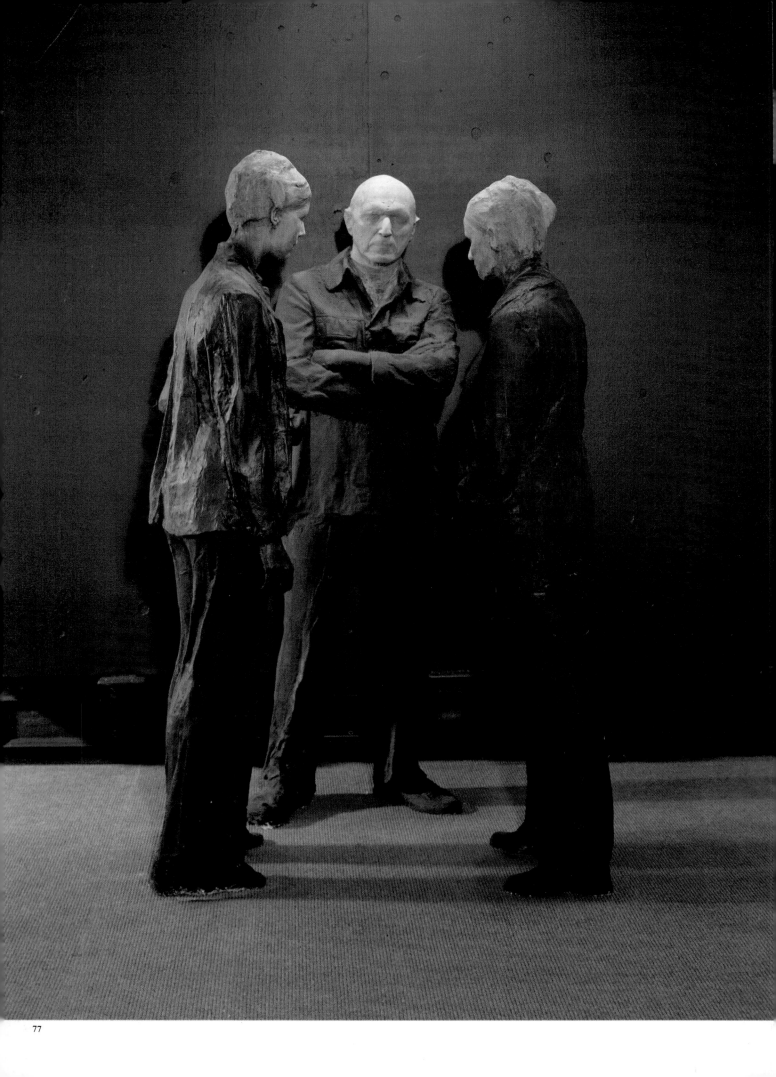

77. *Street Meeting*. 1977.
   Painted plaster and painted wood,
   96×95×52 in. (244×241×132 cm).
   Collection of Bruce and Judith Eissner, Marblehead, Massachussetts.

78. *Girl Sitting on Bed with Bedpost*. 1977.
   Painted plaster and painted wood,
   32×29×20 in. (81×74×52 cm).
   Collection of R. Looker, Carpinteria, California.

79. *Magenta Girl, Blue Door Frame*. 1977.
   Painted plaster and wood,
   43½×22½×8 in. (110×57×20 cm).
   Courtesy of Sidney Janis Gallery, New York.

80. *Flesh Nude in Blue Field I*. 1977.
   Painted plaster, 33½×67½×8 in. (85×171×20 cm).
   Courtesy of Sidney Janis Gallery, New York.

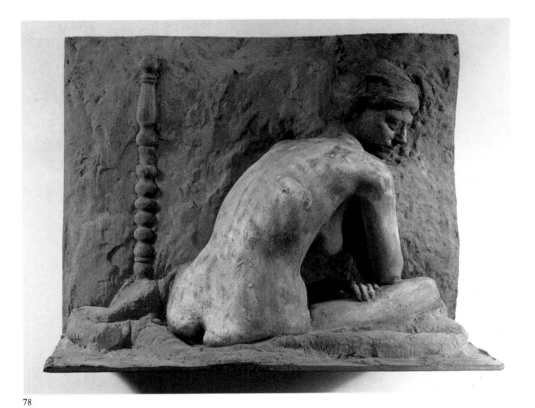

78

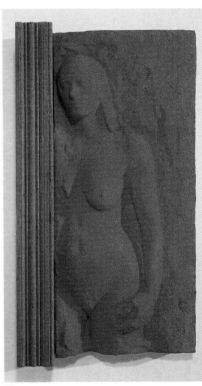

79

80

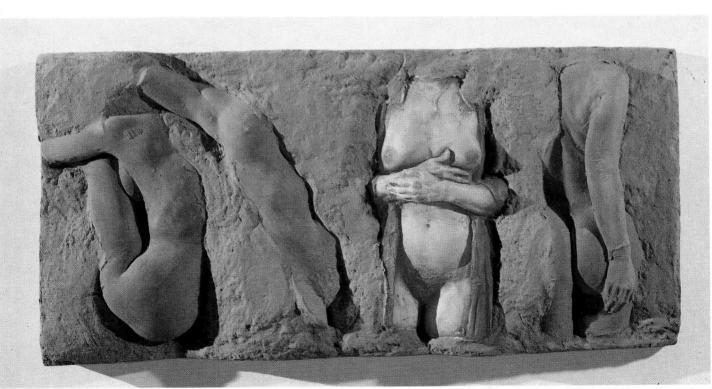

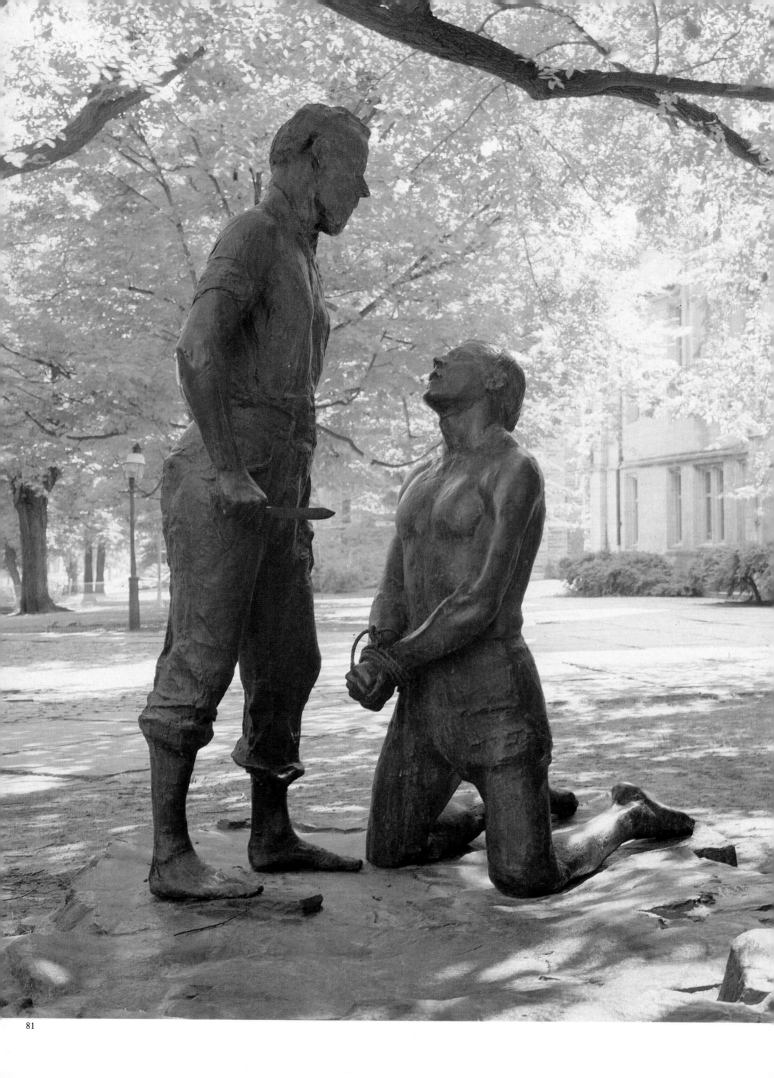

81. *In Memory of May 4, 1970: Kent State - Abraham and Isaac*. 1978.
Bronze, 84×120×50 in. (213×304×127 cm).
John B. Putnam, Jr. Memorial Collection, Princeton University.

82. *Appalachian Farm Couple-1936*. 1978.
Plaster, wood, metal and glass,
108×90×36 in. (274×228×91 cm).
Neuberger Museum, Purchase, New York.

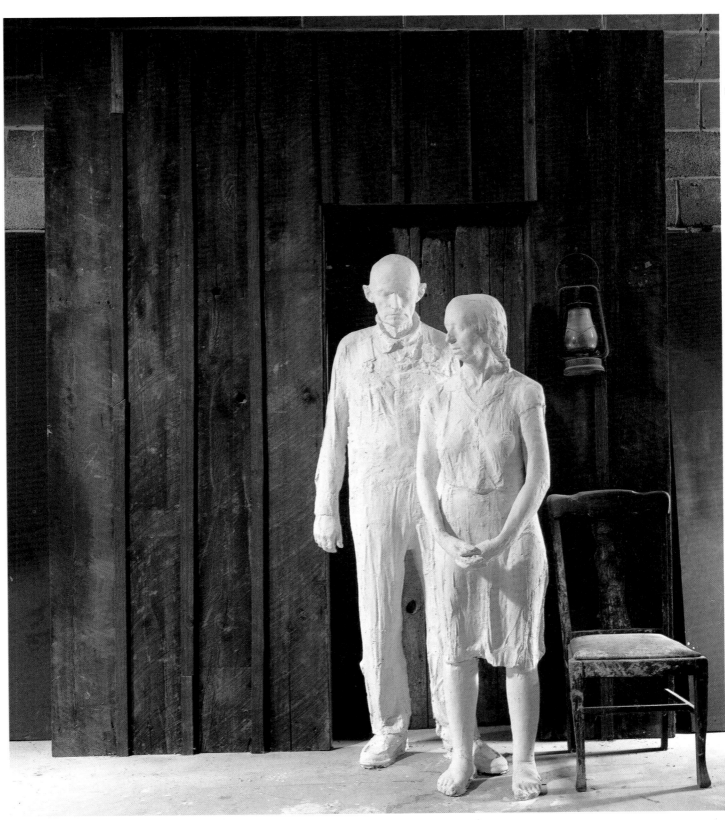

83. *Hot Dog Stand*. 1978.
    Painted plaster, painted wood, plastic, metal and electric lights,
    108 × 72 × 84 in. (274 × 182 × 213 cm).
    San Francisco Museum of Modern Art, San Francisco, California.

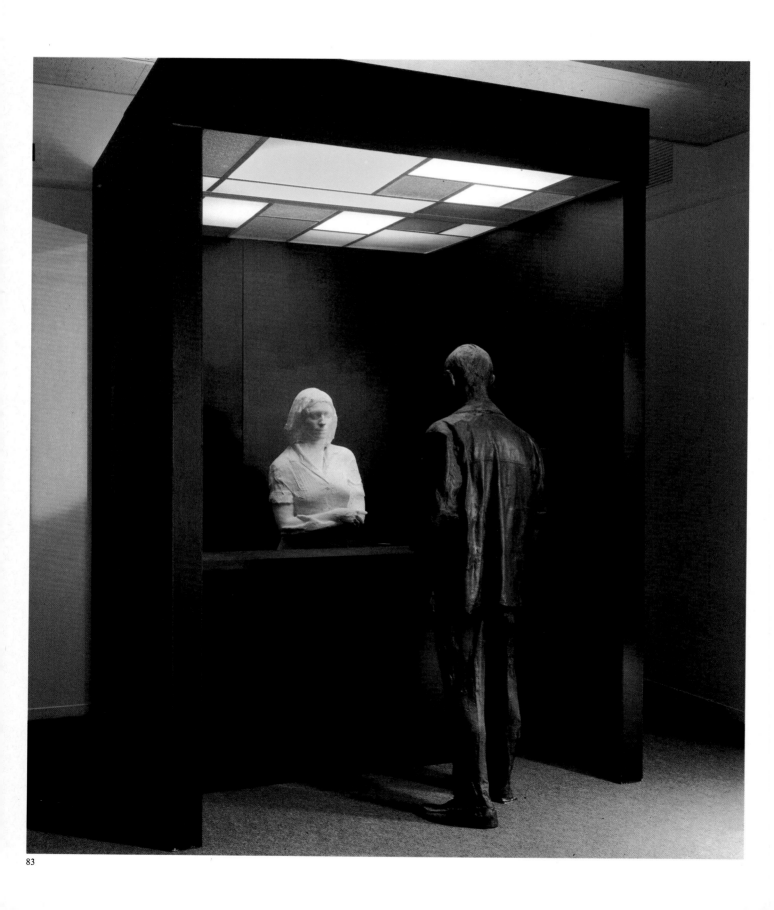

84. *Go-Go Dancer*. 1978.
   Plaster, wood, mirror, electric lights, and vinyl,
   108 × 59 × 48 in. (274 × 150 × 122 cm).
   Collection of Irma and Norma Braman, Miami, Florida.

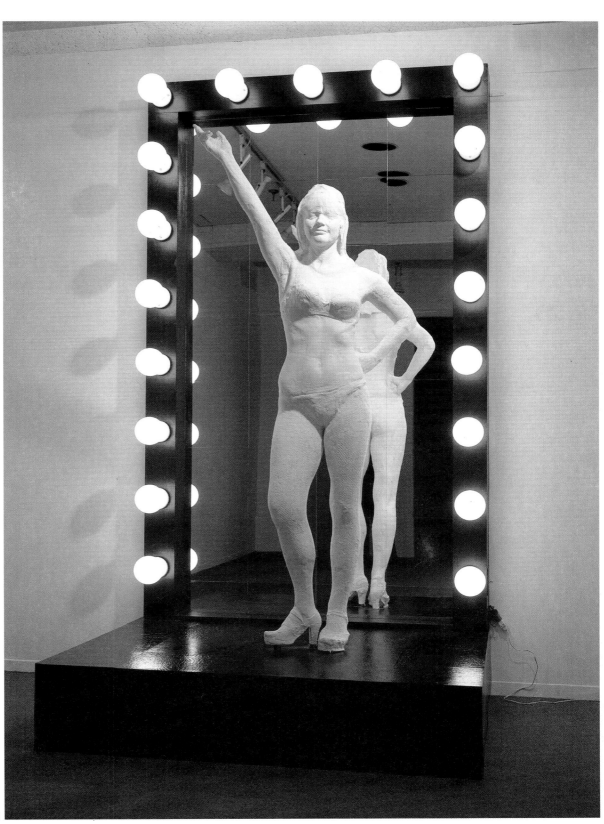

85. *Girl on Blanket, Full Figure.* 1978.
Plaster, 76 × 42 × 12 in. (193 × 107 × 30 cm).
Columbus Museum of Art, Columbus, Ohio.

86. *Blue Girl in Blue Wicker Chair.* 1979.
Painted plaster, 22 × 17 × 8 in. (56 × 43 × 20 cm).
Collection of Jerome Stone, Chicago, Illinois.

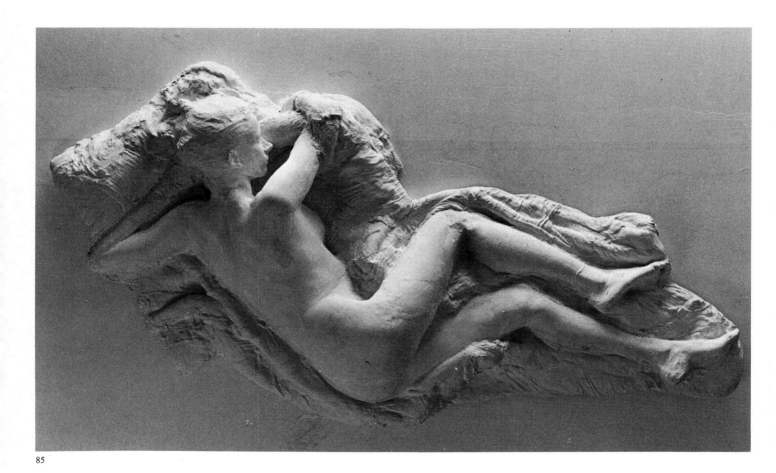

85

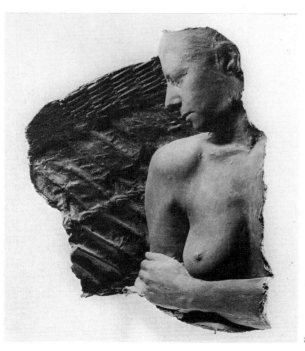

86

87. *Flesh Girl in Blue Wicker Chair*. 1979.
    Painted plaster, 33 × 18 × 15 in. (84 × 46 × 38 cm).
    Courtesy of Sidney Janis Gallery, New York.

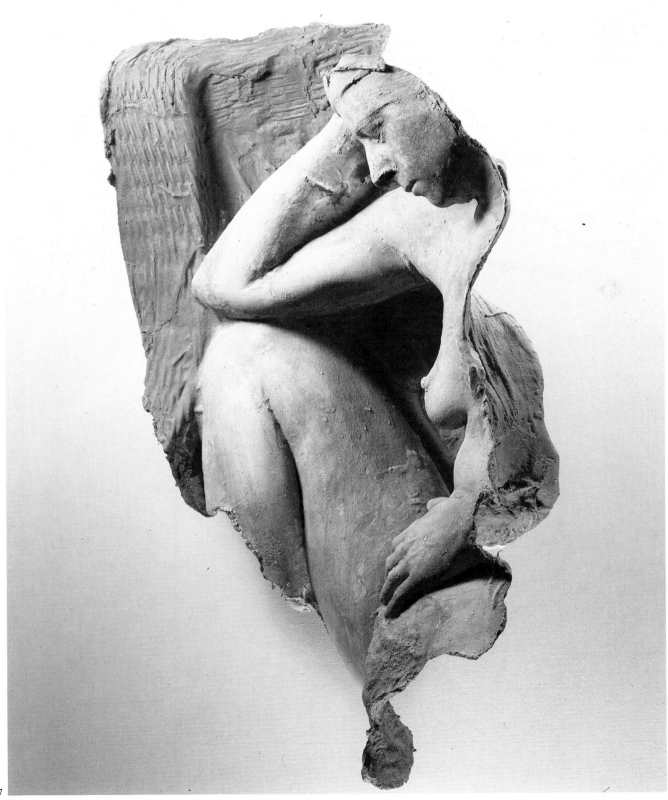

88. *Three People on Four Benches*. 1979.
   Plaster, wood and metal,
   52 × 144 × 58 in. (132 × 366 × 147 cm).
   Sidney Janis Gallery, New York.
   Pepsico Sculpture Gardens, Purchase, New York (A.P.).

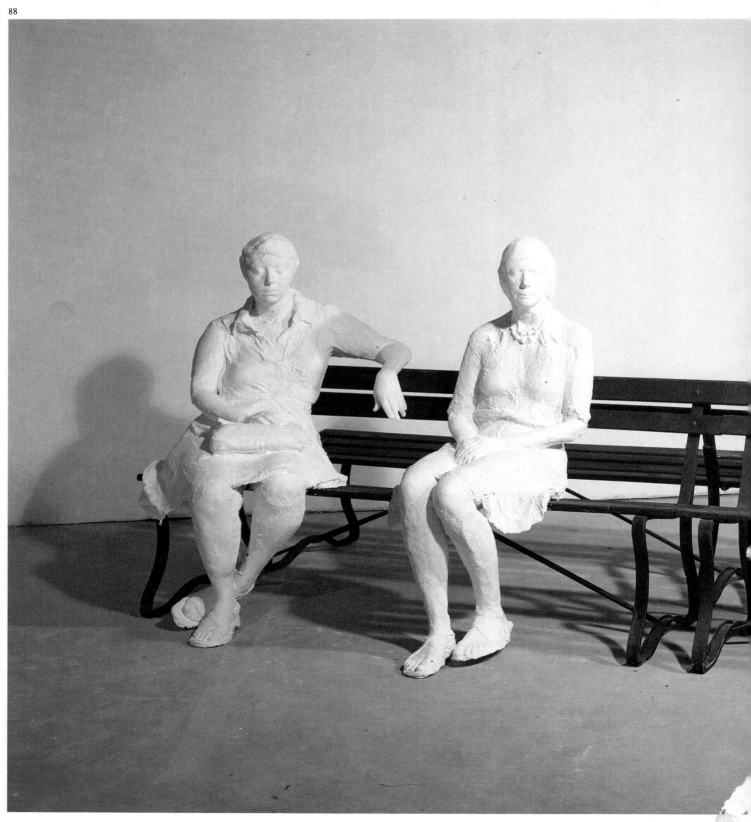

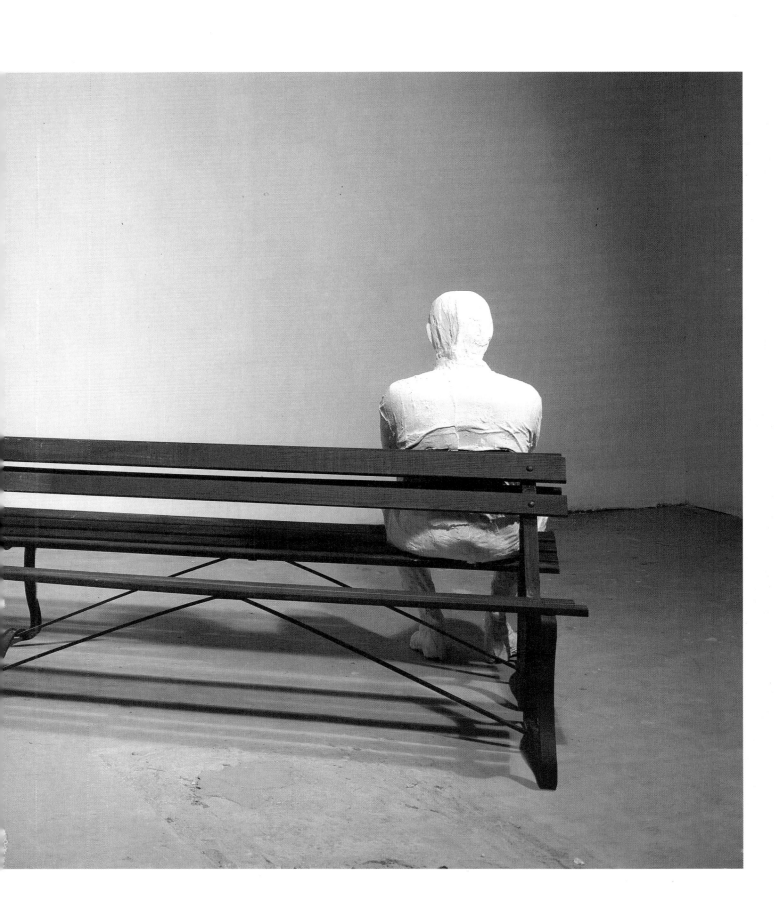

89. *Gay Liberation*. 1980.
    Plaster and metal, 71×192×80 in. (180×488×203 cm).
    The Museum of Modern Art, Seibu Takanawa, Karuizawa, Japan.

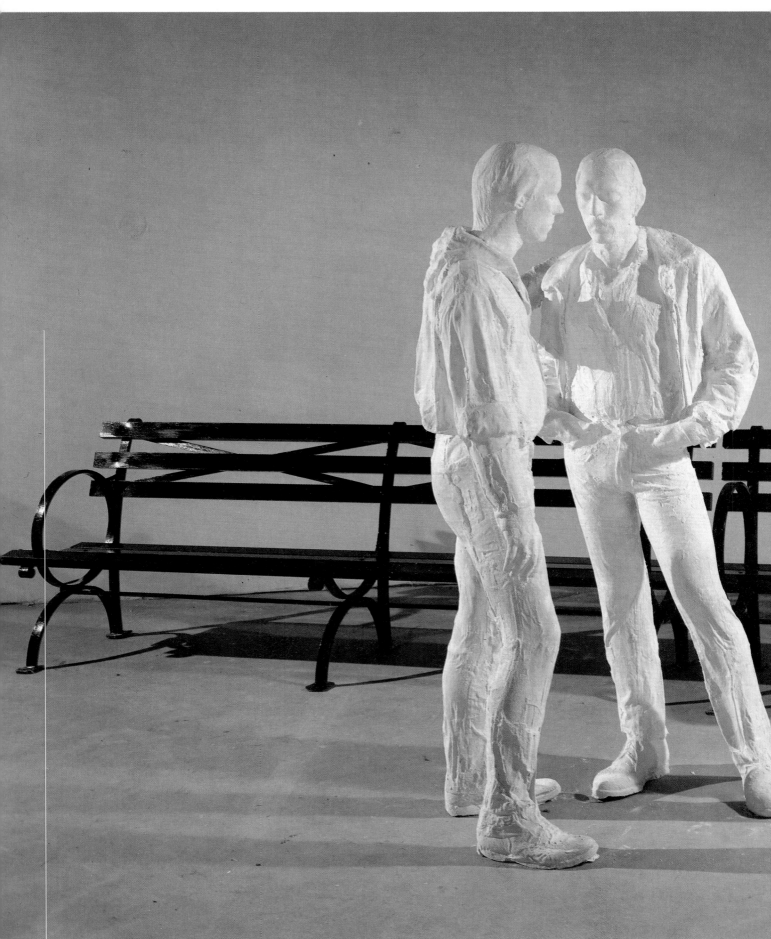

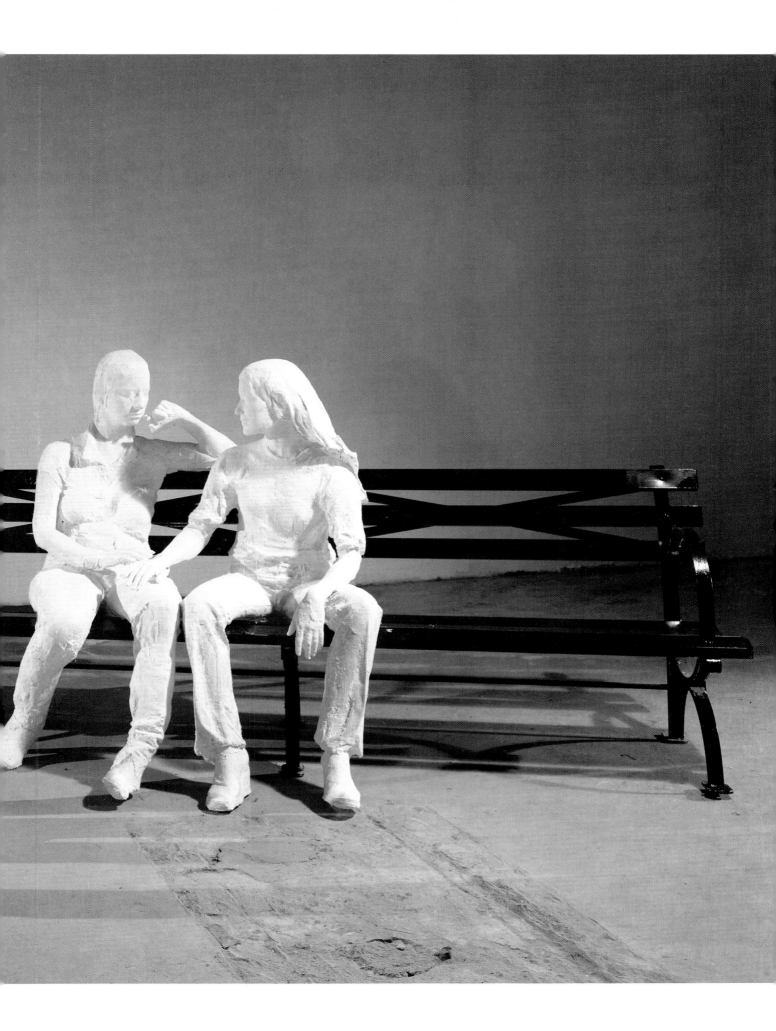

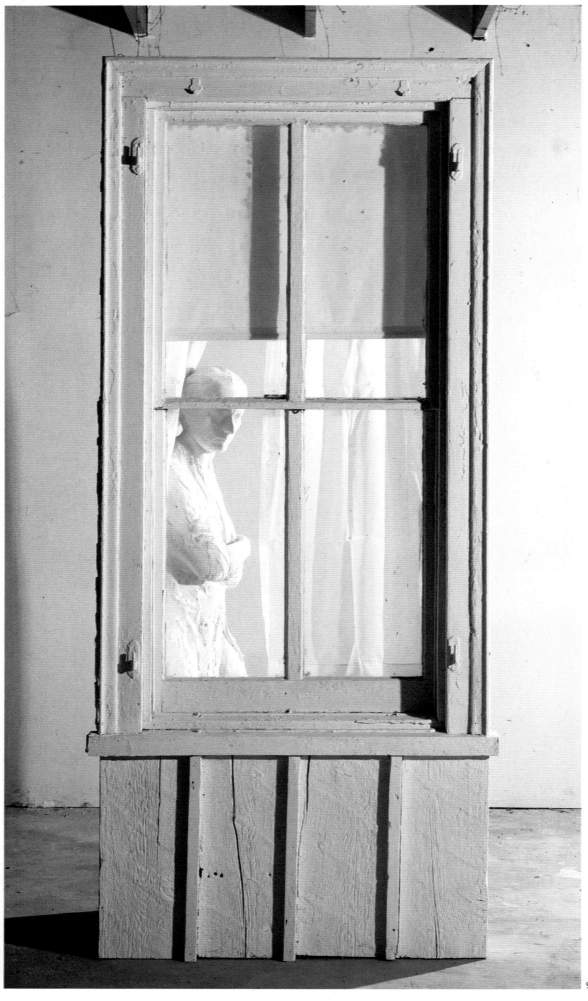

90. *Girl in Kimono Looking Through Window*. 1980. Bronze, glass and plaster, 96 × 43 × 30 in. (244 × 109 × 76 cm). Collection of Mr. and Mrs. Norman Wolgin, Philadelphia, Pennsylvania.

91. *The Steelmakers*. 1980. Plaster, wood, plastic and metal, 120 × 120 × 60 in. (305 × 305 × 152 cm). Courtesy of Sidney Janis Gallery, New York.

92. *Blue Girl on Park Bench*. 1980. Painted plaster and painted aluminum, 51 × 78 × 44 in. (130 × 198 × 111 cm). Collection of Melvin Golder, Melrose Park, Pennsylvania.

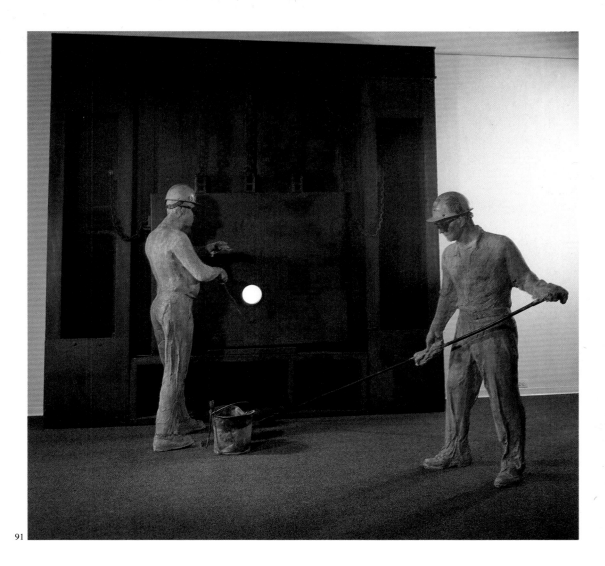

91

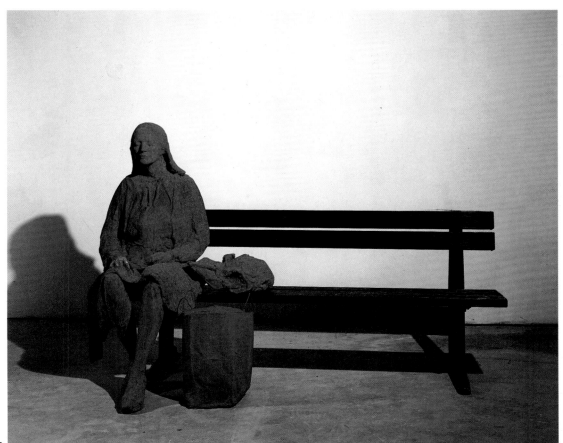

92

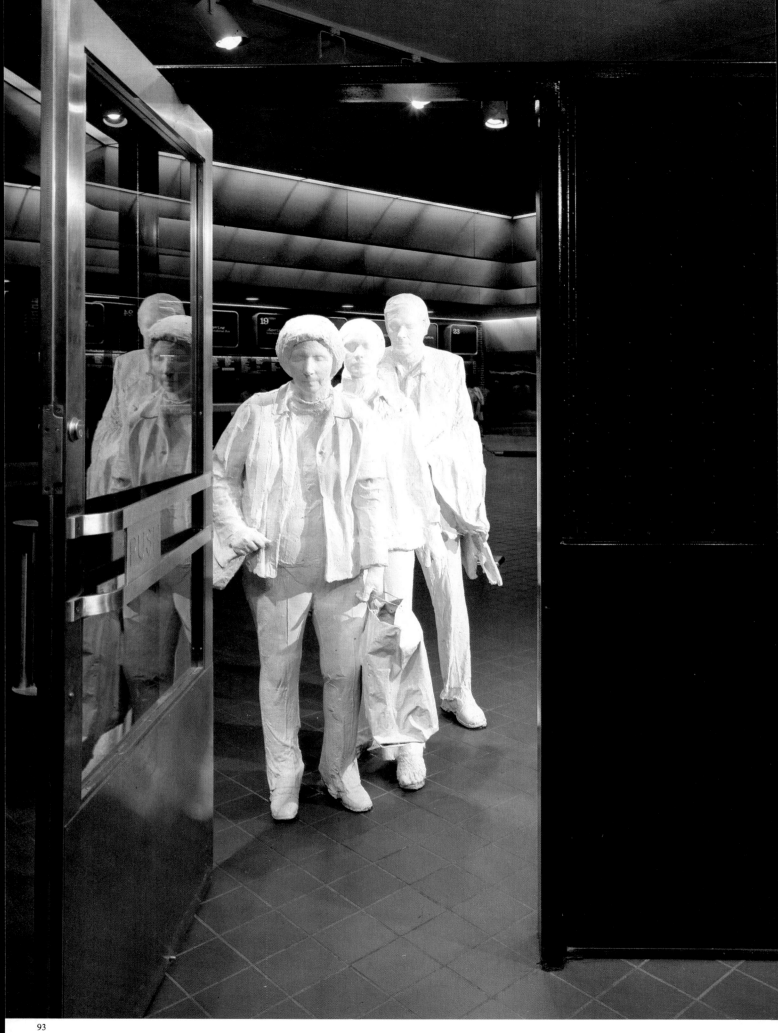

93. *The Commuters*. 1980.
   White bronze, 84 × 72 × 96 in. (213 × 183 × 244 cm).
   Installation at Port Authority Bus Terminal, New York.

94. *The Hustle: The Four-Hand Pass*. 1980.
   Plaster, wood, plastic, videotape and sound/studio,
   96 × 144 × 192 in. (244 × 366 × 488 cm); figures 68 × 38 × 38 in. (173 × 97 × 97 cm).
   Courtesy of Sidney Janis Gallery, New York.

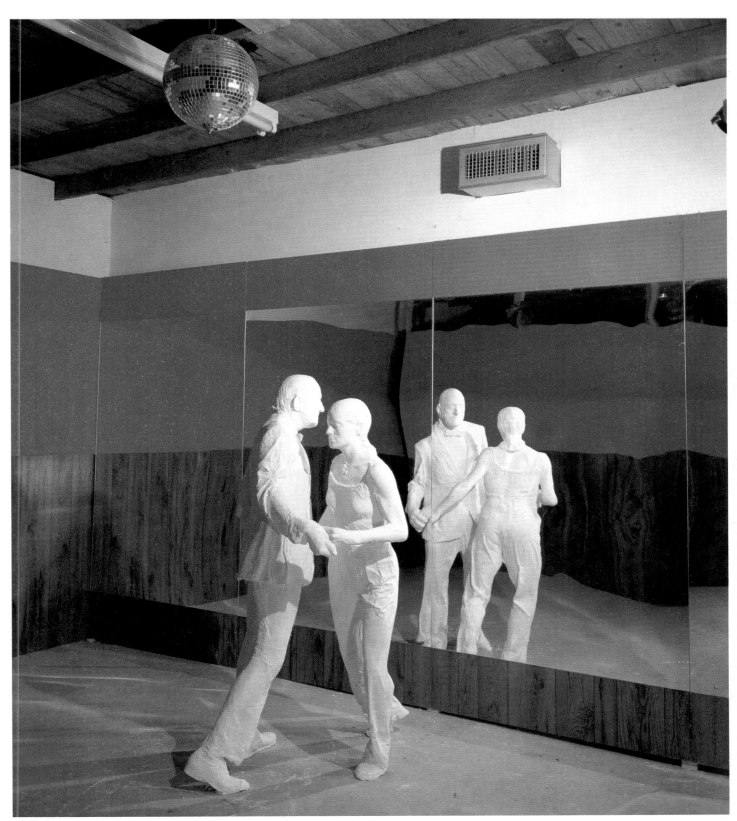

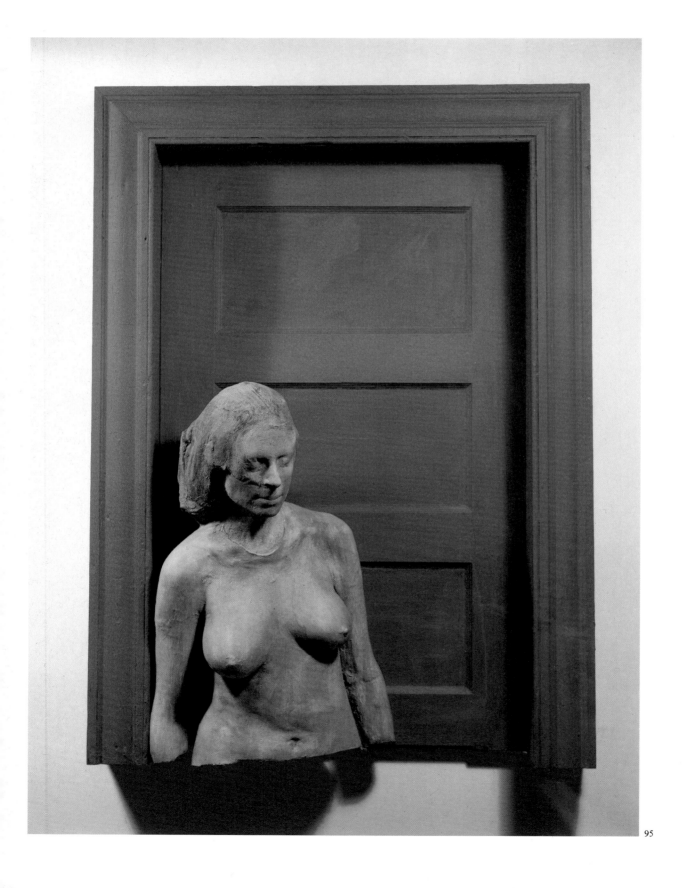

96. *Body Fragment No. 1.* 1980.
Painted plaster, 22¼ × 14 in. (56 × 36 cm).
Collection of Herbert Kohl, Milwaukee, Wisconsin.

97. *Cézanne Still Life No. 2.* 1981.
Painted plaster, wood and metal,
32 × 40 × 18½ in. (81 × 101 × 47 cm).
Courtesy of Sidney Janis Gallery, New York.

98. *Cézanne Still Life No. 3.* 1981.
Painted plaster, wood and metal,
24 × 40 × 27½ in. (61 × 102 × 70 cm).
Courtesy of Sidney Janis Gallery, New York.

99. *Three Bathers with Birch Tree.* 1980.
Plaster and wood,
72 × 64 × 14 in. (183 × 163 × 36 cm).
Collection of Michael Gregory, Wayne, New Jersey.

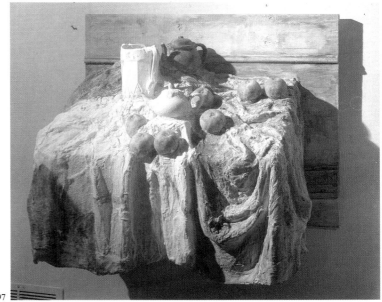

97

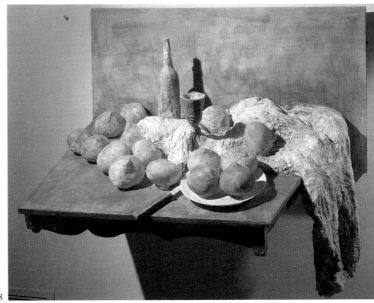

98

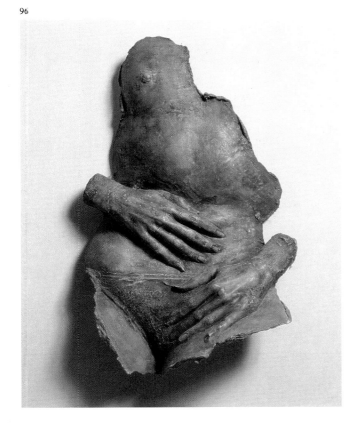

96

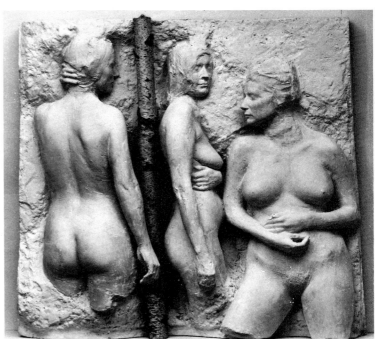

99

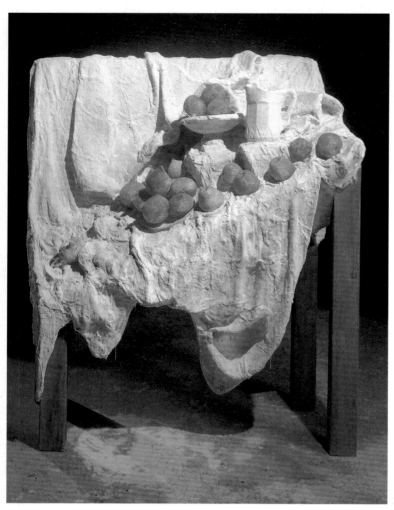

100

100. *Cézanne Still Life No. 4.* 1981.
    Painted plaster, wood and metal,
    57 × 48 × 24 in. (145 × 122 × 61 cm).
    Courtesy of Sidney Janis Gallery, New York.

101. *Woman Eating Apple.* 1981.
    Painted plaster and wood,
    38 × 38 × 8 in. (97 × 97 × 20 cm).
    Courtesy of Sidney Janis Gallery, New York.

102. *Helen with Apples II.* 1981.
    Painted plaster, 96 × 48 × 42 in. (244 × 121 × 107 cm).
    Portland Museum of Art, Portland, Oregon.

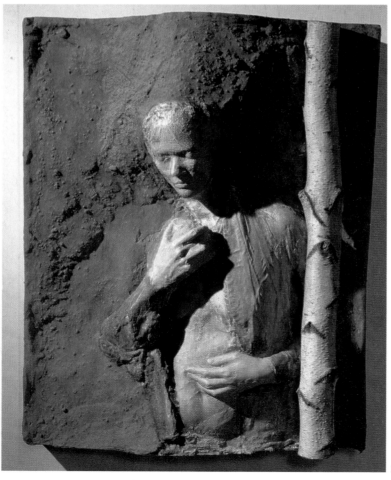

101

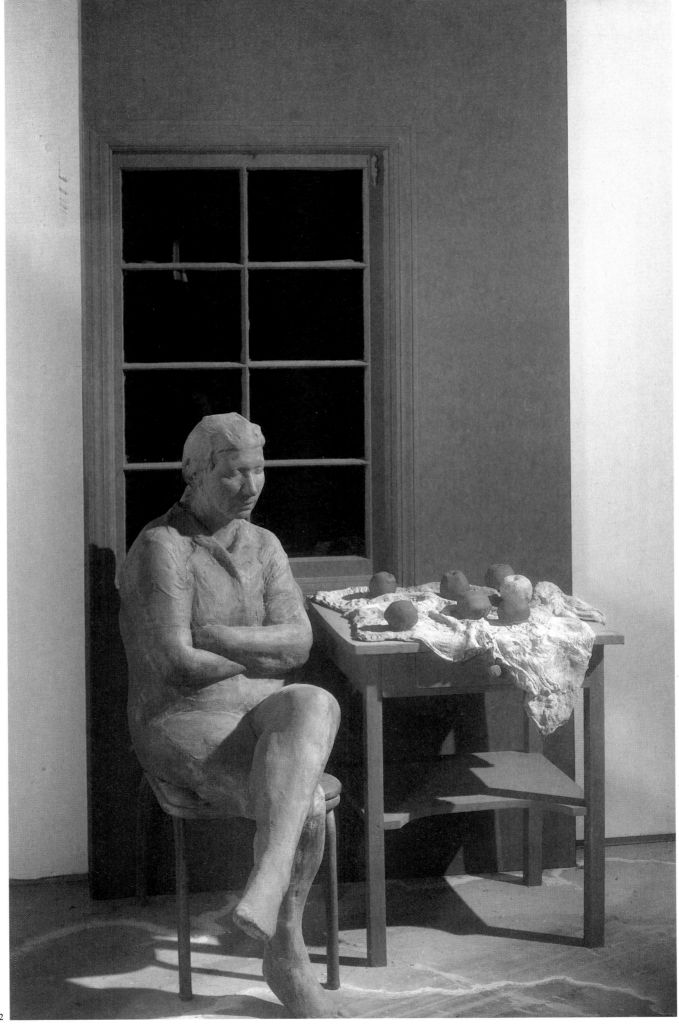

103. *The Circus Flyers*. 1981.
    Plaster, wire and rope,
    72 × 144 × 20 in. (183 × 366 × 51 cm).
    Collection of James H. Binger, Minneapolis, Minnesota,
    for Butler Square.

104. *Woman Standing in Blue Doorway*. 1981.
    Painted plaster and wood,
    82 × 55 × 33 in. (208 × 140 × 84 cm).
    Courtesy of Sidney Janis Gallery, New York.

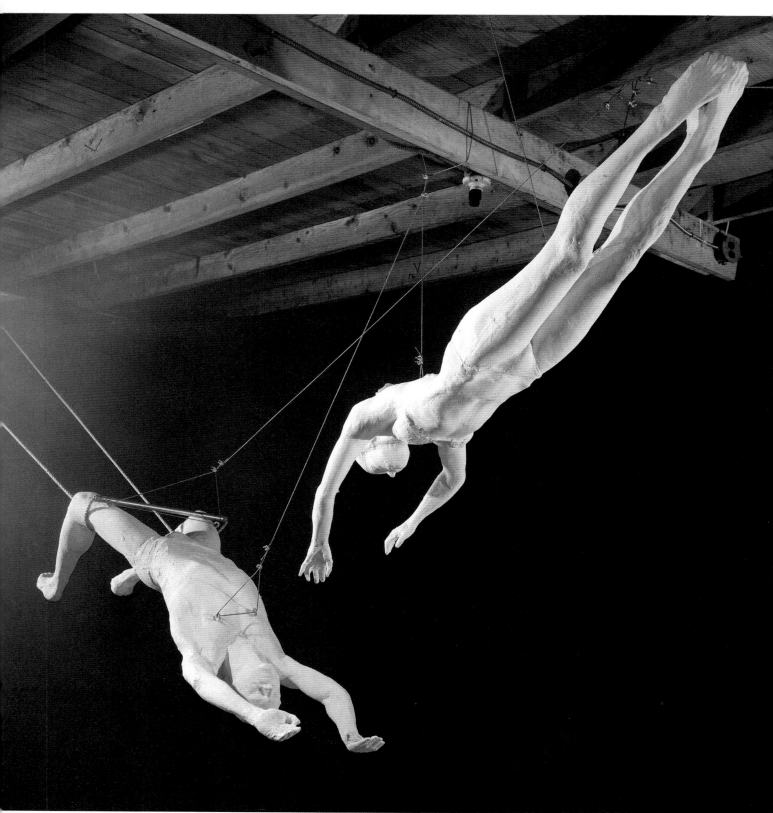

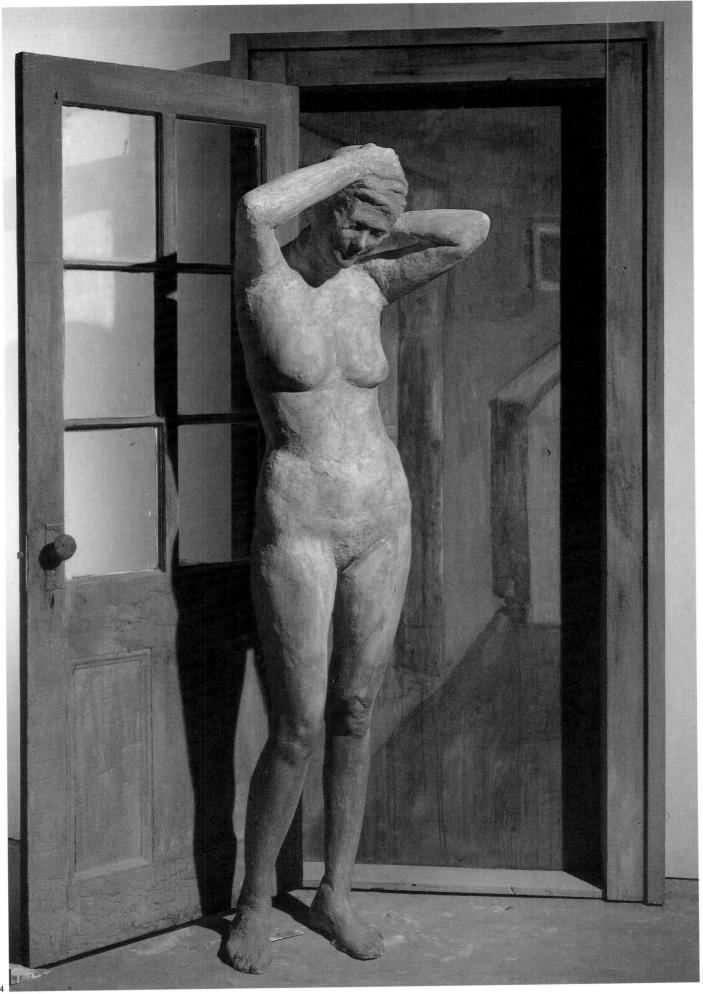

105. *The Holocaust*. 1983.
Plaster and mixed media,
120×240×120 in. (305×610×305 cm).
Courtesy of Sidney Janis Gallery, New York.

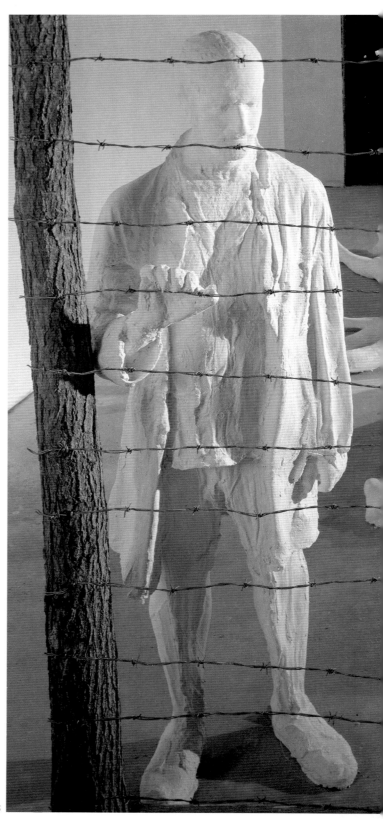

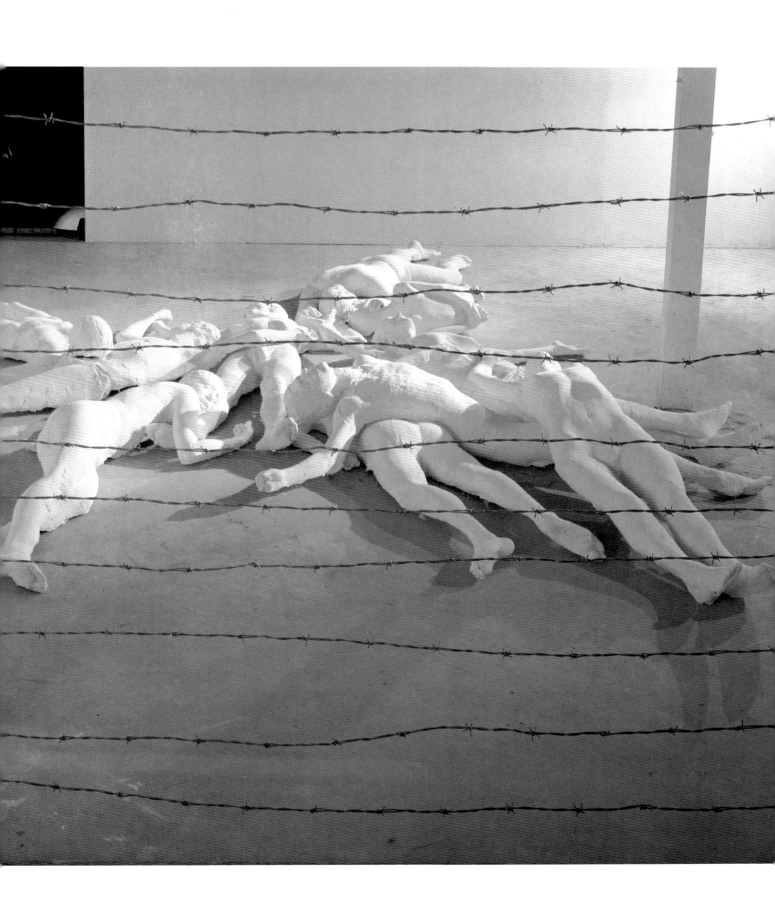

106. *Machine of the Year*. 1983.
(*Time* magazine cover)
Plaster, wood, plastic and mixed media,
96 × 144 × 96 in. (244 × 366 × 244 cm).
Collection of Time-Life Inc., New York.

107. *Rush Hour*. 1983.
Plaster, 96 × 96 × 192 in. (244 × 244 × 488 cm).
Courtesy of Sidney Janis Gallery, New York.

108. *Jacob and the Angels*. 1984.
Plaster, wood, plastic and rock,
132 × 144 × 76 in. (335 × 366 × 193 cm).
Courtesy of Sidney Janis Gallery, New York.

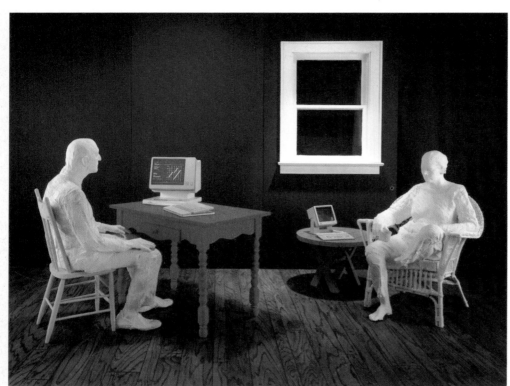

106

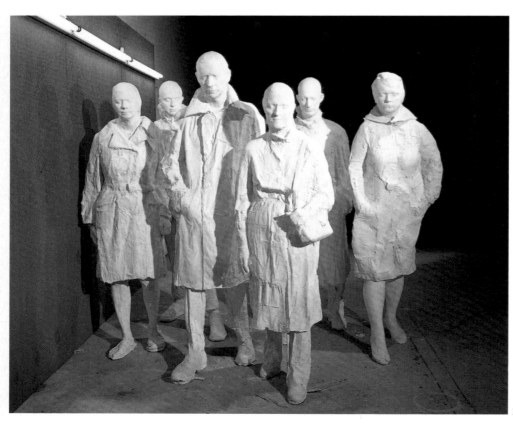

107

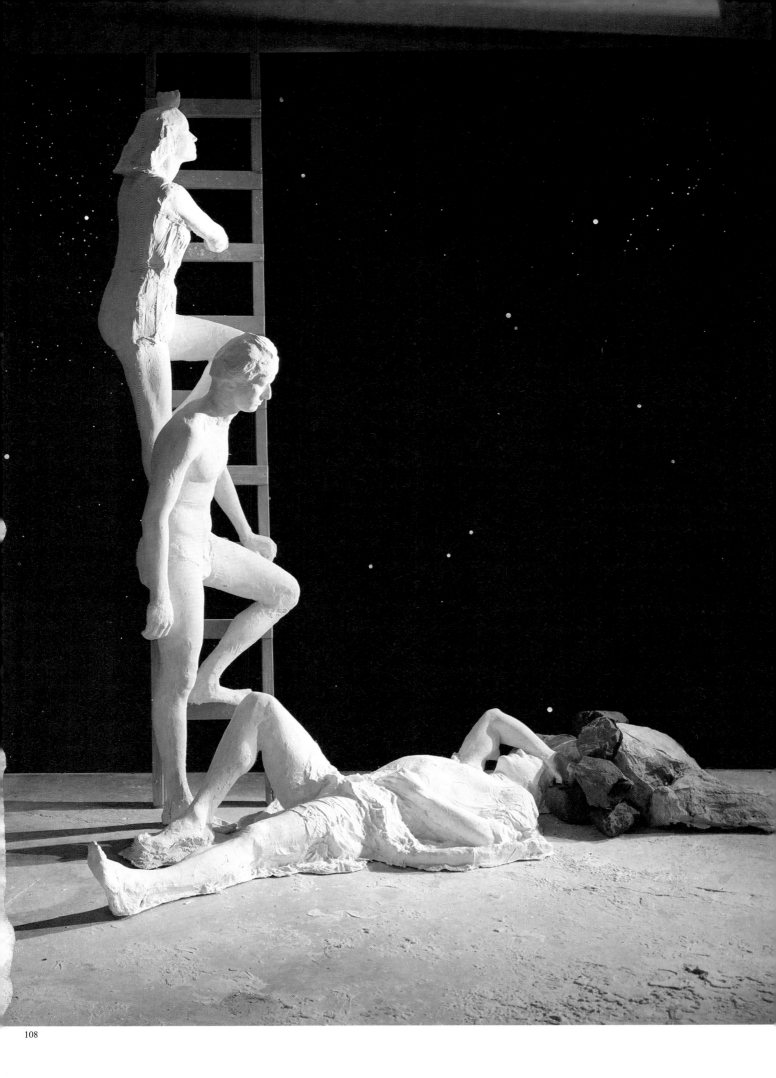

109. *Woman on Orange Bed*. 1984.
Painted plaster, 44 × 56 × 76 in. (112 × 142 × 193 cm).
Courtesy of Sidney Janis Gallery, New York.

110. *Ruben's Women*. 1984.
Plaster and mixed media,
84 in. high (213 cm).
Courtesy of Sidney Janis Gallery, New York.

111. *Portrait of Mayor Teddy Kolleck*. 1984.
Plaster and wood chair,
53 × 29 × 35 in. (135 × 74 × 89 cm).
Courtesy of Sidney Janis Gallery, New York.

112. *Nude on Redwood Chaise*. 1985.
Painted plaster and mixed media,
35 × 67 × 37 in. (89 × 170 × 94 cm).
Courtesy of Sidney Janis Gallery, New York.

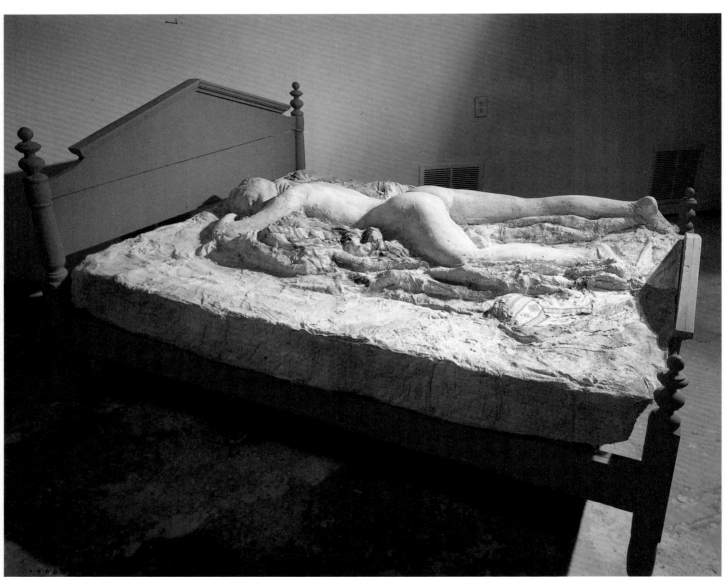

109

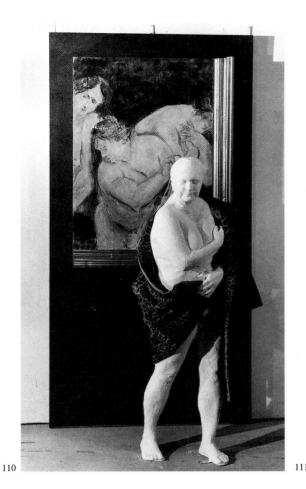

110

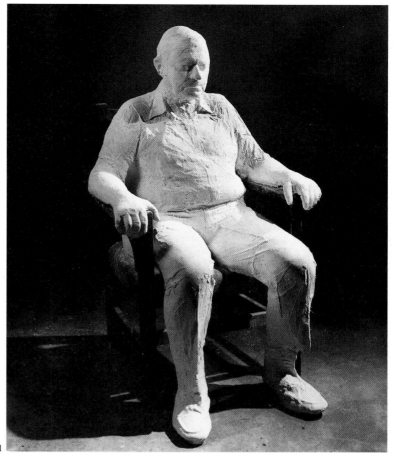

111

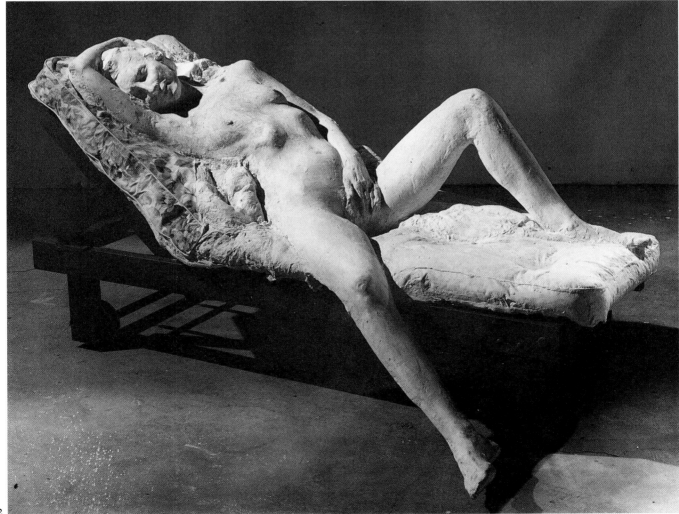

112

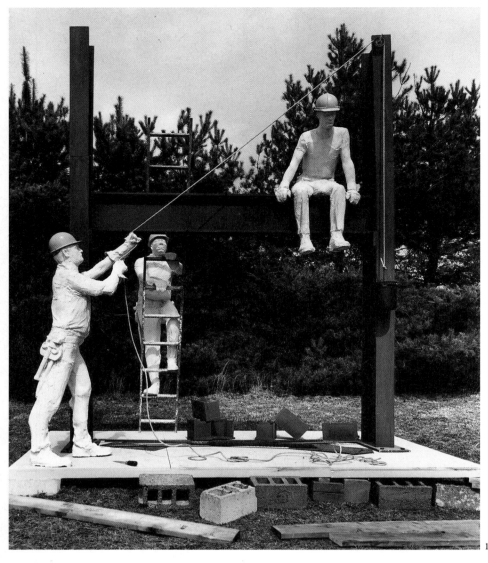

113

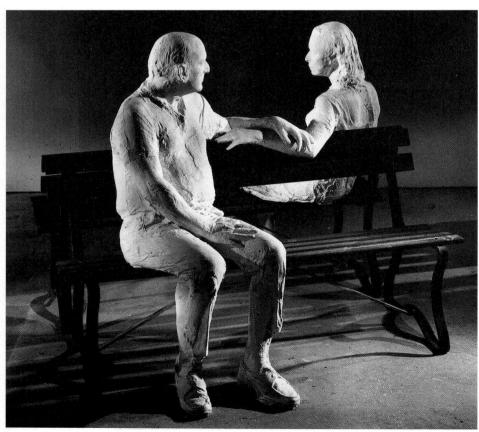

114

113. *The Constructors*. 1985 (work-in-progress).
Plaster and mixed media,
13½ × 12 × 7 ft. (4 × 3.5 × 2.13 m).
The Mary Roebling Building, State Department
of Commerce, Trenton, New Jersey.

114. *Couple on Two Benches*. 1985.
Plaster and bench,
51 × 62 × 62 in. (130 × 157 × 157 cm).
Courtesy of Sidney Janis Gallery, New York.

115. *Still Life with Pipe, Chair & Apples* (Braque). 1985.
Plaster, wood, and paint,
42 × 57 × 6 in. (107 × 145 × 15 cm).
Richard Gray Gallery, Chicago, Illinois.

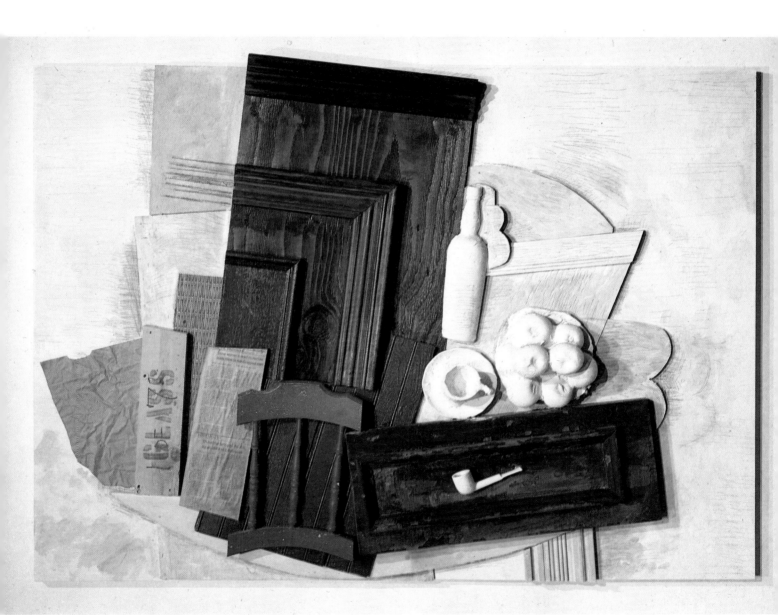

115

116. *Still Life with Shoe & Rooster* (Braque). 1986.
Plaster, wood and paint,
52 × 36½ × 27½ in. (132 × 93 × 69 cm).
Courtesy of Sidney Janis Gallery, New York.

117. *Man with Guitar* (Picasso). 1986.
Plaster, wood and paint,
61 × 31 × 9 in. (155 × 79 × 23 cm).
Courtesy of Sidney Janis Gallery, New York.

118. *Portrait of Jacob Javits*. 1986.
Painted plaster and wood,
96 × 44¼ × 43 in. (244 × 112 × 109 cm).
Courtesy of Sidney Janis Gallery, New York.

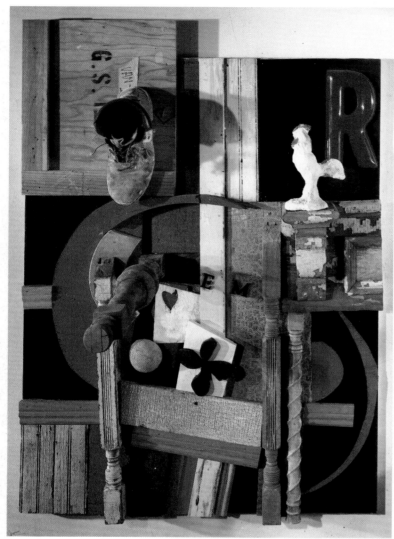

116

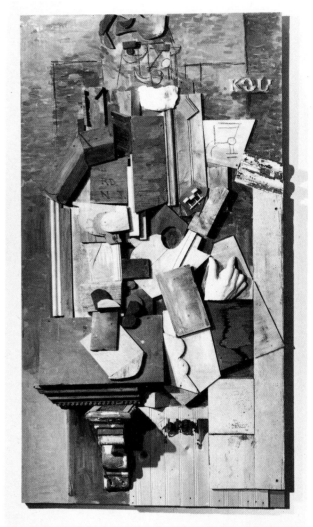

117

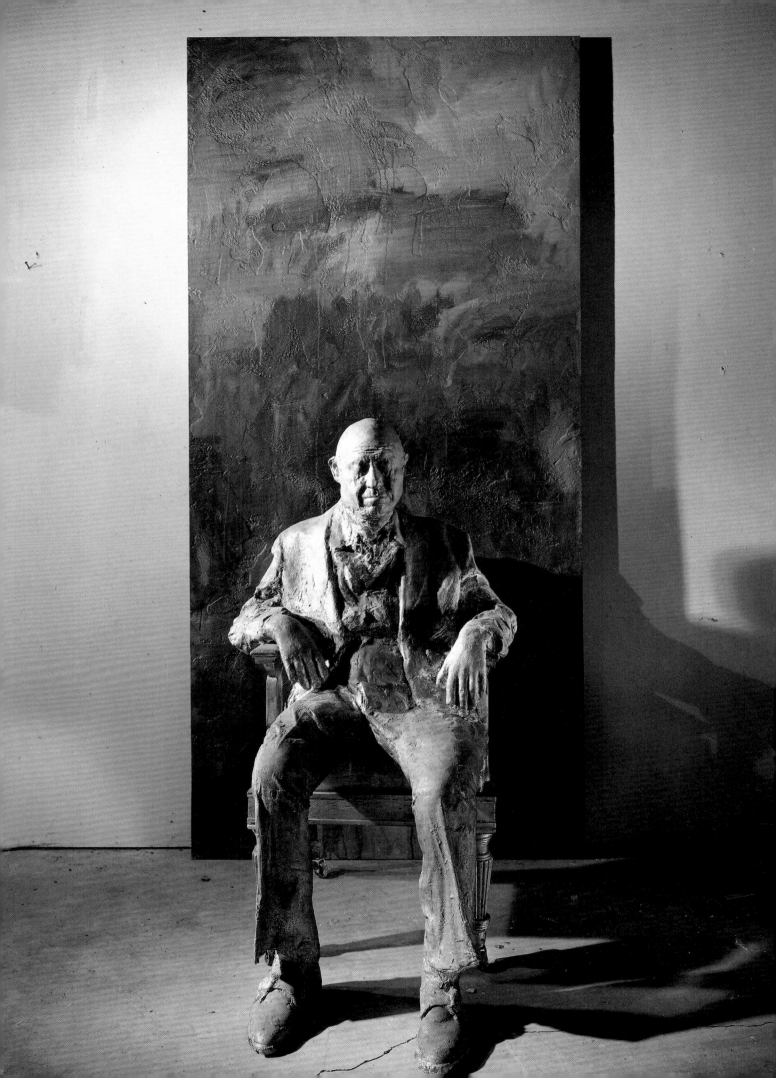

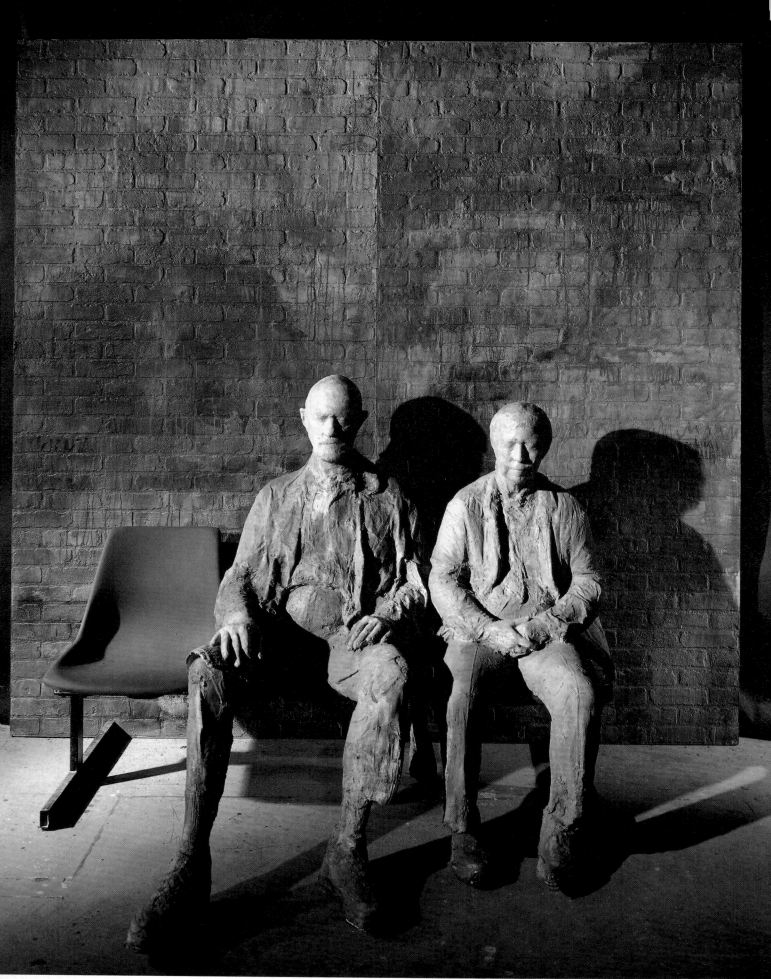

119. *Couple Against Gray Brick Wall*. 1986.
Painted plaster and wood,
96 × 96 × 51 in. (244 × 244 × 130 cm).
Courtesy of Sidney Janis Gallery, New York.

120. *Woman Seated on Chair with Caning*. 1987.
Plaster, wood and mixed media,
59 × 37 × 10 in. (150 × 94 × 25 cm).
Courtesy of Sidney Janis Gallery, New York.

121. *Lot's Wife*. 1987.
Plaster, and mixed media,
53 × 53 × 18 in. (135 × 135 × 46 cm).
Courtesy of Sidney Janis Gallery, New York.

122. *Helen Against Wall with Door*. 1987.
Painted plaster and wood,
38 × 55 × 14 in. (97 × 140 × 36 cm).
Courtesy of Sidney Janis Gallery, New York.

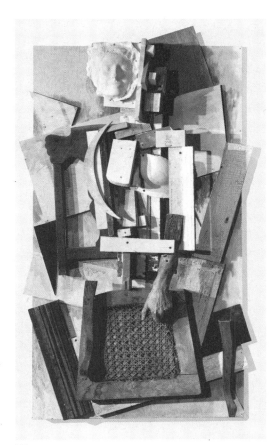

120

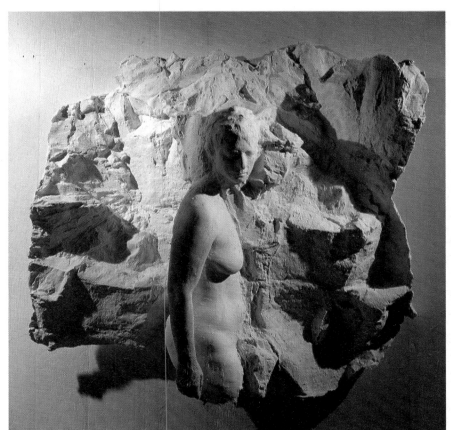

121

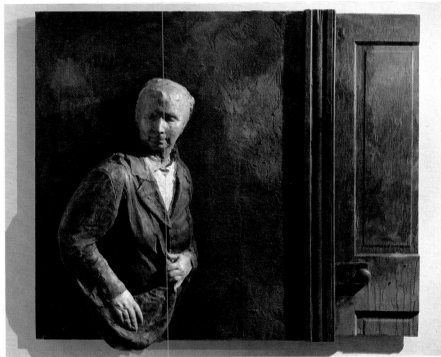

122

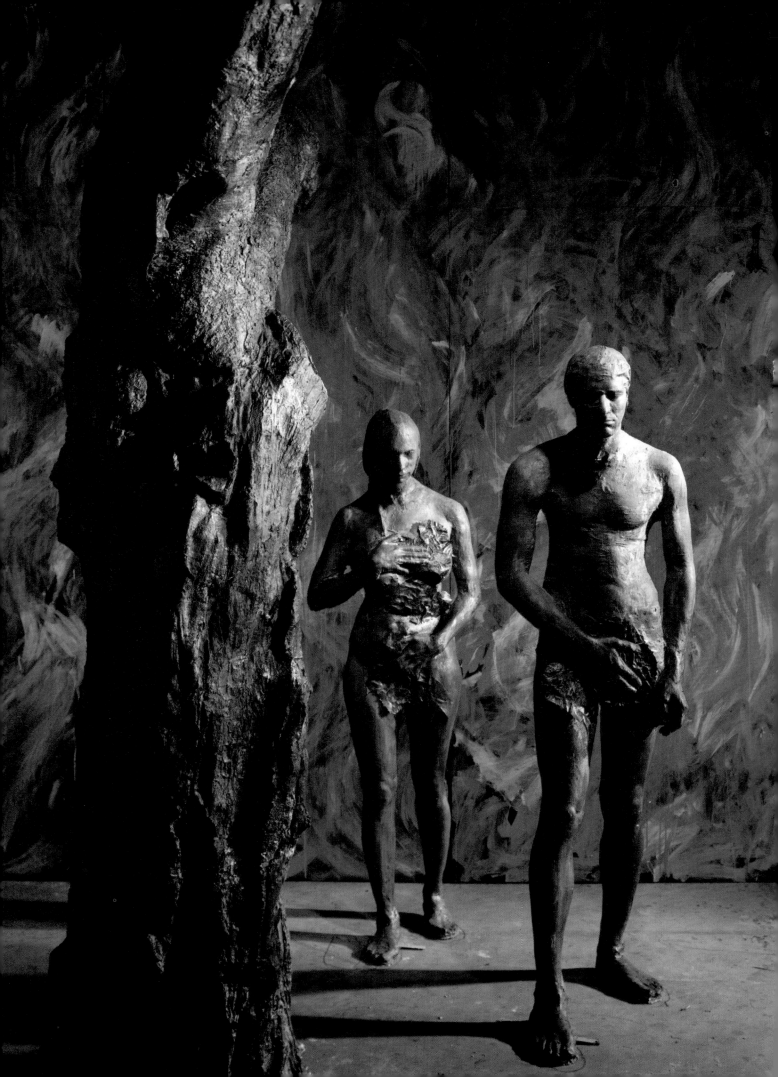

123. *The Expulsion*. 1986-1987.
    Painted plaster, 126 × 144 × 84 in. (320 × 366 × 213 cm).
    Courtesy of Sidney Janis Gallery, New York.

124. *Abraham's Farewell to Ishmael*. 1987.
    Painted plaster, 102 × 78 × 78 in. (259 × 198 × 198 cm).
    Courtesy of Sidney Janis Gallery, New York.

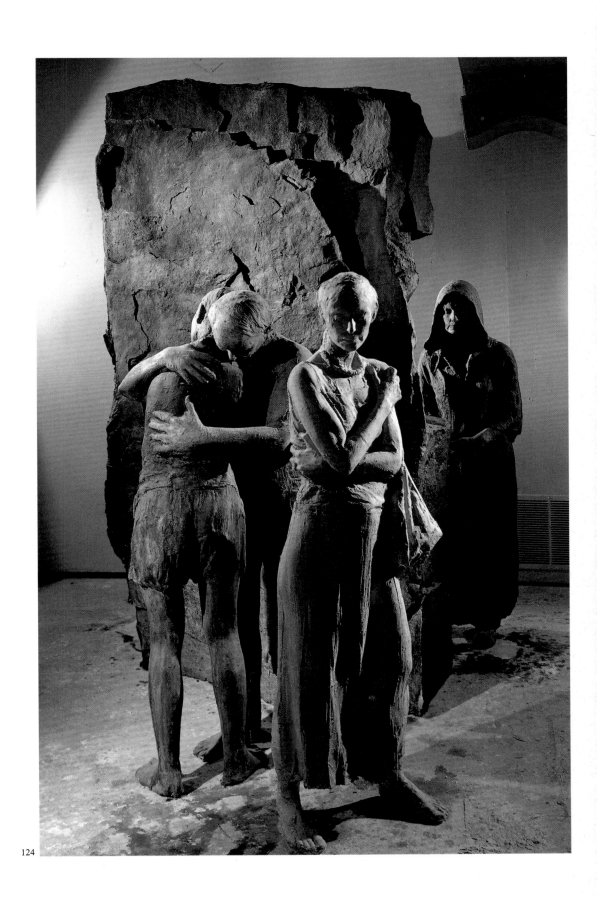

125. *The Street*. 1987.
Painted plaster, wood, and mixed media,
8 ft. 6 in. × 26 ft. × 6 ft. (2.59 × 7.92 × 1.83 m).
Courtesy of Sidney Janis Gallery, New York.

125

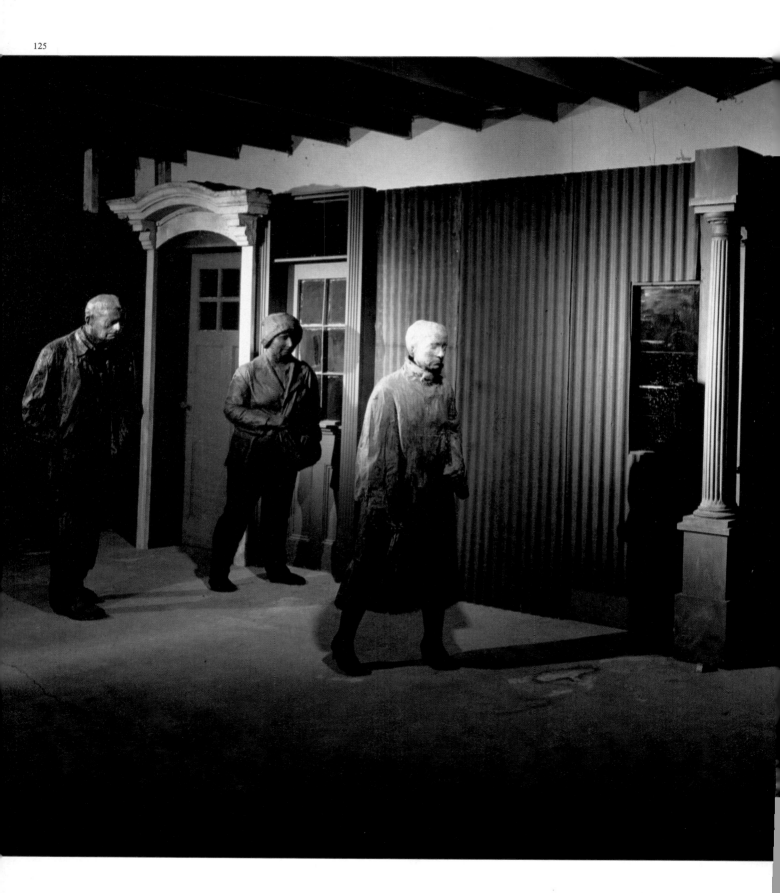

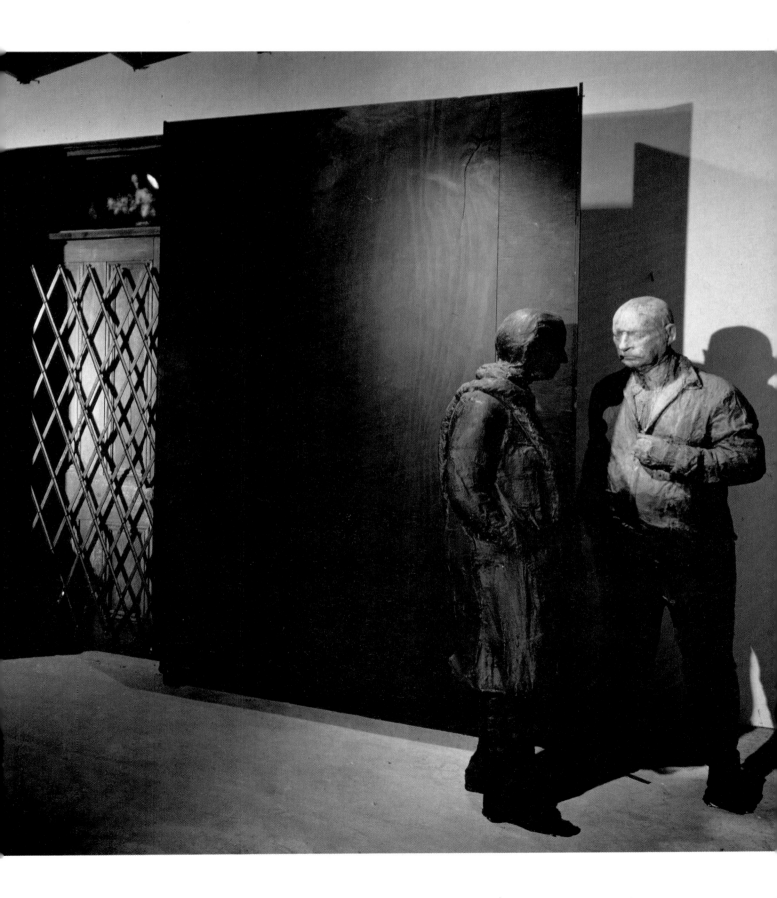

TABLE OF ILLUSTRATIONS

1. *Legend of Lot*. 1958.
Oil on canvas, plaster, wood and chicken
wire, 72×96 in. (183×244 cm).
Collection of the artist.

2. *Man on a Bicycle I*. 1958-1959.
Wood, metal and rubber,
65×58×24 in. (165×147×71 cm).
Collection of the artist.

3. *Bas-relief: Nude*. 1958.
Plaster, 36×66×3 in. (91×167×7.5 cm).
Collection of the artist.

4. *Man Sitting at a Table*. 1961.
Plaster, wood and glass, 53×48×48 in.
(135×122×122 cm).
Städtische Kunsthalle Mannheim, Germany.

5. *Lovers on a Bed I*. 1962.
Plaster, wood, metal, mattress and cloth,
48×54×70 in. (122×137×178 cm).
Collection of Mrs. Robert B. Mayer,
Chicago.

6. *Woman Shaving Her Leg*. 1963.
Plaster, metal, porcelain and Masonite,
63×65×30 in. (160×165×76 cm).
Collection of Mrs. Robert B. Mayer,
Chicago.

7. *Cinema*. 1963.
Plaster, metal, Plexiglas and fluorescent
light, 118×96×39 in. (300×244×99 cm).
Albright-Knox Art Gallery, Buffalo (Gift of
Seymour H. Knox).

8. *Man Leaning on a Car Door*. 1963.
Plaster, wood and metal, 96×48×30 in.
(244×122×76 cm).
Staatsgalerie Stuttgart, Stuttgart.

9. *The Gas Station*. 1963-1964.
Plaster, metal, glass, stone and rubber,
96×264×60 in. (244×671×152 cm).
The National Gallery of Canada, Ottawa.

10. *The Artist's Studio*. 1963.
Plaster, wood, metal, paint and mixed
media, 96×72×108 in. (244×183×274 cm).
Harry N. Abrams Family Collection,
New York.

11. *The Bus Station*. 1965.
Plaster, wood an plastic, 96×48×24 in.
(244×122×61 cm).
Collection of Howard and Jean Lipman,
New York.

12. *The Dry Cleaning Store*. 1964.
Plaster, wood, metal, aluminum paint and
neon tubing, 96×108×86 in.
(244×274×218 cm).
Moderna Museet, Stockholm.

13. *Rock and Roll Combo*. 1964.
Plaster, wood, tiling and musical
instruments, 84×84×69 in.
(213×213×175 cm).
Hessisches Landesmuseum, Darmstadt,
Germany (Collection of Karl Stroher).

14. *Woman in a Doorway I*. 1964.
Plaster, wood, glass and aluminum paint,
113×63¼×18 in. (287×161×46 cm).
Whitney Museum of American Art,
New York.

15. *Robert and Ethel Scull*. 1965.
Plaster, wood, canvas and cloth,
96×72×72 in (244×183×183 cm).
Collection of Mr. and Mrs. Robert C. Scull,
New York.

16. *The Butcher Shop*. 1965.
Plaster, metal, wood, vinyl, Plexiglas and
other objects, 94×99¼×48 in.
(239×252×122 cm).
Art Gallery of Ontario, Toronto
(Gift from the Women's Committee Fund,
1966).

17. *The Diner*. 1964-1966.
Plaster, wood, metal Formica, Masonite and
fluorescent light, 102×108×87 in.
(259×274×221 cm).
Walker Art Center, Minneapolis, Minnesota.

18. *Woman Washing Her Foot in a Sink*.
1965.
Plaster, wood metal and porcelain,
60×48×36 in. (152.5×122×91.5 cm).
Wallraf-Richartz-Museum, Cologne
(Ludwig Collection).

19. *The Billboard*. 1966.
Plaster, wood, metal and rope,
189×117×20 in. (480×297×51 cm).
South Mall Project, Albany.

20. *John Chamberlain Working*. 1965-1967.
Plaster, metal, plastic and aluminum paint,
69×66×56 in (175×168×142 cm).
The Museum of Modern Art, New York
(Promised gift of Carroll Janis and Conrad
Janis).

21. *Walking Man*. 1966.
Plaster, wood and painted metal,
84×58×34 in. (214×147×86 cm).
Collection of Mrs. Norman B. Champ, Jr.,
Saint Louis.

22. *The Truck*. 1966.
Plaster, wood, metal, glass, vinyl and film
projector, 66×60×53 in.
(168×152×135 cm).
Art Institute of Chicago (Mr. and Mrs.
Frank G. Logan Fund).

23. *The Execution*. 1967.
Plaster, wood, metal and rope,
96×132×96 in. (244×335×244 cm).
Vancouver Art Gallery.

24. *The Parking Garage*. 1968.
Plaster, wood, metal, electrical parts and
light bulbs, 120×152×48 in.
(305×386×122 cm).
Newark Museum, New Jersey.

25. *Man Leaving a Bus*. 1967.
Plaster, painted metal, glass, chrome and
rubber, 88½×39×33½ in. (225×99×85 cm).
Harry N. Abrams Family Collection,
New York.

26. *The Moviehouse*. 1966-1967.
Plaster, wood, plastic and incandescent
lights, 102×148×153 in.
(259×376×388 cm).
Musée National d'Art Moderne, Paris
(on loan from Centre National d'Art
Contemporain, Paris).

27. *Sidney Janis with Mondrian's
"Composition" of 1933, on an Easel*. 1967.
Plaster, wood, metal and canvas,
67×50×33 in. (170×127×84 cm).
The Museum of Modern Art, New York
(Sidney and Harriet Janis Collection).

28. *Artist in His Studio*. 1968.
Plaster, wood, paper and pastel,
96×120×108 in. (244×305×274 cm).
Collection of Reinhard Onnasch, Berlin.

29. *Girl Sitting Against a Wall I*. 1968.
Plaster, wood and glass, 84×96×37 in.
(213×244×94 cm).
Staatsgalerie Stuttgart, Stuttgart.

30. *The Subway*. 1968.
Plaster, metal, glass, rattan, incandescent
light and electrical parts, 90×115×53 in.
(229×292×135 cm).
Collection of Mrs. Robert B. Mayer,
Chicago.

31. *Construction Tunnel*. 1968.
Plaster, wood and metal, 168×60×93 in.
(427×153×236 cm).
The Detroit Institute of Arts (Founders
Society Purchase).

32. *The Artist in His Loft*. 1969.
Plaster, wood, metal, glass and porcelain,
90×69×60 in. (229×175×152 cm).
Collection of Reinhard Onnasch, Berlin.

33. *Self-Portrait with Head and Body*. 1968.
Plaster and wood, 66×32×42 in.
(168×81×107 cm).
Collection of Carter Burden, New York.

34. *Box: Man in a Bar*. 1969.
Plaster, wood, metal and cloth,
60×24×12 in. (152×70×30 cm).
Collection of Mr. and Mrs. E. A. Bergman,
Chicago.

35. *Box: Woman Looking Through
Window*. 1969.
Plaster, wood, and celotex, 60×24×12 in.
(152×70×30 cm).
Collection of Serge de Bloe, Brussels.

36. *The Brick Wall*. 1970.
Plaster, wood and plastic, 96×152×42 in.
(244×386×107 cm).
Gatodo Gallery, Tokyo, Japan.

37. *Lovers on a Bed II*. 1970.
Plaster and metal, 48×72×60 in.
(122×183×152 cm). Phillip Johnson
Collection, New York.

38. *Girl Walking Out of the Ocean*. 1970.
Plaster and wood, 84×60×28½ in.
(213×152×72 cm).
Private collection, Brussels.

39. *The Aerial View*. 1970.
Plaster, wood, plastic, incandescent and
fluorescent light, 96×105×48 in.
(244×267×121 cm).
The Art Museum of the Atenaeum, Helsinki
(Collection Sara Hilden).

40. *Alice Listening to Her Poetry and
Music*. 1970.
Plaster, wood, glass and tape recorder,
96×96×33 in. (244×244×84 cm).
Staatsgalerie Moderner Kunst, Munich.

41. *Times Square at Night*. 1970.
Plaster, wood, plastic, incandescent and
fluorescent light, 108 × 96 × 60 in.
(274 × 244 × 152 cm).
Joslyn Art Museum, Omaha, Nebraska.

42. *The Bowery*. 1970.
Plaster, wood and metal, 96 × 96 × 72 in.
(244 × 244 × 183 cm).
Kunsthaus, Zurich.

43-44. *The Bar*. 1971.
Plaster, wood, metal, glass, plastic, neon
light and television, 96 × 102 × 36 in.
(243 × 259 × 91.5 cm).
Collection of Martin Z. Margulies, Grove
Isle, Florida.

45. *The Dancers*. 1971.
Bronze, 72 × 144 × 96 in. (183 × 366 × 244 cm).
National Gallery of Art, Washington, D.C.
(2/5).

46. *To All Gates*. 1971.
Plaster, wood, metal, plastic and fluorescent
light, 96 × 144 × 96 in. (244 × 366 × 244 cm).
Des Moines Art Center (Coffin Fine Arts
Trust Fund).

47. *Man Standing on a Printing Press*. 1971.
Plaster, wood and metal, 96 × 96 × 24 in.
(244 × 244 × 70 cm).
Des Moines Register & Tribune Company,
Des Moines, Iowa.

48. *Girl Looking Through Window*. 1972.
Plaster and mixed media, 96 × 36 × 24 in.
(244 × 91 × 70 cm).
Museum Boymans-van Beuningen,
Rotterdam.

49. *The Costume Party* (Final Version).
1965-1972.
Acrylic on plaster, metal, wood and mixed
media, 72 × 144 × 108 in. (183 × 366 × 274 cm).
Courtesy of Sidney Janis Gallery, New York.

50. *The Red Light*. 1972.
Plaster and mixed media, 114 × 96 × 36 in.
(290 × 244 × 91 cm).
Cleveland Museum of Art (Andrew R. and
Martha Holden Jennings Fund).

51. *Picasso's Chair*. 1973.
Plaster and mixed media, 78 × 60 in.
(198 × 152 cm).
Guggenheim Museum, New York.

52. *Girl on Blanket: Hand on Leg*. 1973.
Plaster, 50 × 39 × 10 in. (127 × 99 × 25 cm).
Collection of Mr. and Mrs. Robert Kardon,
Philadelphia, Pennsylvania.

53. *Girl on Red Wicker Couch*. 1973.
Plaster and mixed media, 35 × 80 × 58 in.
(89 × 203 × 147 cm).
Hopkins Center Art Gallery, Dartmouth
College, Hanover, New Hampshire.

54. *Girl Drying Her Knee*. 1973.
Plaster, aluminum and cloth, 59 × 24 × 44 in.
(150 × 70 × 112 cm).
Collection of Ercole Lauro, Naples.

55. *Waitress Pouring Coffee*. 1973.
Plaster, wood, metal and porcelain,
96 × 42 × 34 in (244 × 107 × 86 cm).
Shiga Museum of Art, Otsu, Japan.

56. *Girl on Red Chair with Blue Robe*.
1974.
Plaster, wood and acrylic, 96½ × 48 × 45 in.
(245 × 122 × 114 cm).
Collection of Leonard and Gloria Luria,
Miami, Florida.

57. *Girl in Robe I*. 1974.
Plaster, 33 × 14½ × 8 in. (84 × 37 × 20 cm).
Courtesy of Sidney Janis Gallery, New
York.

58. *Girl in Robe III*. 1974.
Plaster, 36¼ × 18 × 9 in. (92 × 46 × 23 cm).
Collection of D. Makler Gallery,
Philadelphia, Pennsylvania.

59. *Girl Seated on Gray Chair*. 1974.
Plaster, wood and plastic, 36 × 26⅛ × 20¾ in.
(91 × 66 × 52 cm).
Courtesy of Sidney Janis Gallery, New York.

60. *The Blue Robe*. 1974.
Plaster and cloth, 49 × 36¾ × 14½ in.
(124 × 93 × 37 cm).
Courtesy of Sidney Janis Gallery, New York.

61. *Girl Emerging from Tile Wall*. 1974.
Plastic and ceramic tile, 39 × 16⅜ × 10 in.
(99 × 42 × 25 cm).
Collection of Barry Boonshaft, Quakertown,
Pennsylvania.

62. *Embracing Couple*. 1975.
Plaster, 34 × 30¾ × 11½ in. (86 × 78 × 29 cm).
Martin Friedman, Walker Art Center,
Minneapolis, Minnesota.

63. *Two Torsos*. 1975.
Plaster, 41 × 30 × 9 in. (104 × 76 × 23 cm).
Collection of Robert Weiss, Chicago,
Illinois.

64. *Girl Next to Chimney* (Version 1). 1975.
Plaster, wood and plastic, 32½ × 40 × 11½ in.
(83 × 102 × 29 cm).
Courtesy of Sidney Janis Gallery, New York.

65. *The Corridor*. 1975.
Plaster and wood, 84 × 84 × 48 in.
(213 × 213 × 122 cm).
Tamayo Museum, Mexico City, Mexico.

66. *Exit*. 1975.
Plaster, wood, plastic and electric light,
84 × 72 × 36 in (213 × 182 × 91.5 cm).
Philadelphia Museum of Art (Gift of the
Friends of the Philadelphia of Art Museum).

67. *The Restaurant*. 1976.
Bronze, brick, cement, steel, aluminum,
tempered glass, and fluorescent light,
120 × 192 × 96 in. (305 × 488 × 244 cm).
Federal Office Building, Buffalo.

68. *Girl Standing in Nature*. 1976.
Bronze, 67 in. high (170 cm).
Collection of City of Greenwich,
Connecticut.

69. *Post No Bills*. 1976.
Work destroyed.

70. *Black Girl Behind Red Door*. 1976.
Painted plaster and wood, 82 × 38 × 24 in.
(208 × 97 × 61 cm).
Collection of Madame Landau, Paris.

71. *Walk, Don't Walk*. 1976.
Plaster, cement, metal, painted wood and
electric light, 104 × 72 × 72 in.
(264 × 183 × 183 cm).
Whitney Museum of American Art,
New York.

72. *Red Girl Behind Red Door*. 1976.
Painted plaster and wood, 91 × 50 × 25 in.
(231 × 127 × 64 cm).
Collection of Irma and Norman Braman,
Miami, Florida.

73. *Couple on Black Bed*. 1976.
Painted plaster and wood, 44 × 82 × 60 in.
(112 × 208 × 152 cm).
Collection of Sydney and Frances Lewis
Foundation, Virginia.

74. *Flesh Nude in Blue Field II*. 1977.
Painted plaster and wood, 37¾ × 16½ × 7½ in.
(96 × 42 × 19 cm).
Courtesy of Sidney Janis Gallery, New York.

75. *Magenta Girl on Green Door*. 1977.
Painted plaster and wood,
72½ × 23 × 12 in. (184 × 58 × 30 cm).
Dr. Milton D. Ratner Family Collection.

76. *Brown Girl*. 1977.
Painted plaster, 35 × 12 × 10½ in.
(89 × 30 × 27 cm).
Courtesy of Sidney Janis Gallery, New York.

77. *Street Meeting*. 1977.
Painted plaster and painted wood,
96 × 95 × 52 in. (244 × 241 × 132 cm).
Collection of Bruce and Judith Eissner,
Marblehead, Massachussetts.

78. *Girl Sitting on Bed with Bedpost*. 1977.
Painted plaster and painted wood,
32 × 29 × 20 in. (81 × 74 × 52 cm).
Collection of R. Looker, Carpinteria,
California.

79. *Magenta Girl, Blue Door Frame*. 1977.
Painted plaster and wood, 43½ × 22½ × 8 in.
(110 × 57 × 20 cm).
Courtesy of Sidney Janis Gallery, New York.

80. *Flesh Nude in Blue Field I*. 1977.
Painted plaster, 33½ × 67½ × 8 in.
(85 × 171 × 20 cm).
Courtesy of Sidney Janis Gallery, New York.

81. *In Memory of May 4, 1970: Kent State -
Abraham and Isaac*. 1978.
Bronze, 84 × 120 × 50 in. (213 × 304 × 127 cm).
John B. Putnam, Jr. Memorial Collection,
Princeton University.

82. *Appalachian Farm Couple-1936*. 1978.
Plaster, wood, metal and glass,
108 × 90 × 36 in. (274 × 228 × 91 cm).
Neuberger Museum, Purchase, New York.

83. *Hot Dog Stand*. 1978.
Painted plaster, painted wood, plastic, metal
and electric lights, 108 × 72 × 84 in.
(274 × 182 × 213 cm).
San Francisco Museum of Modern Art, San
Francisco, California.

84. *Go-Go Dancer*. 1978.
Plaster, wood, mirror, electric lights, and
vinyl, 108 × 59 × 48 in. (274 × 150 × 122 cm).
Collection of Irma and Norma Braman,
Miami, Florida.

85. *Girl on Blanket, Full Figure.* 1978.
Plaster, 76 × 42 × 12 in. (193 × 107 × 30 cm).
Columbus Museum of Art, Columbus,
Ohio.

86. *Blue Girl in Blue Wicker Chair.* 1979.
Painted plaster, 22 × 17 × 8 in.
(56 × 43 × 20 cm).
Collection of Jerome Stone, Chicago,
Illinois.

87. *Flesh Girl in Blue Wicker Chair.* 1979.
Painted plaster, 33 × 18 × 15 in.
(84 × 46 × 38 cm).
Courtesy of Sidney Janis Gallery, New York.

88. *Three People on Four Benches.* 1979.
Plaster, wood and metal, 52 × 144 × 58 in.
(132 × 366 × 147 cm).
Sidney Janis Gallery, New York.
Pepsico Sculpture Gardens, Purchase,
New York (A.P.).

89. *Gay Liberation.* 1980.
Plaster and metal, 71 × 192 × 80 in.
(180 × 488 × 203 cm).
The Museum of Modern Art, Seibu
Takanawa, Karuizawa, Japan.

90. *Girl in Kimono Looking Through
Window.* 1980.
Bronze, glass and plaster, 96 × 43 × 30 in.
(244 × 109 × 76 cm).
Collection of Mr. and Mrs. Norman Wolgin,
Philadelphia, Pennsylvania.

91. *The Steelmakers.* 1980.
Plaster, wood, plastic and metal,
120 × 120 × 60 in. (305 × 305 × 152 cm).
Courtesy of Sidney Janis Gallery,
New York.

92. *Blue Girl on Park Bench.* 1980.
Painted plaster and painted aluminum,
51 × 78 × 44 in. (130 × 198 × 111 cm).
Collection of Melvin Golder, Melrose Park,
Pennsylvania.

93. *The Commuters.* 1980.
White bronze, 84 × 72 × 96 in.
(213 × 183 × 244 cm).
Installation at Port Authority Bus Terminal,
New York.

94. *The Hustle: The Four-Hand Pass.* 1980.
Plaster, wood, plastic, videotape and
sound/studio, 96 × 144 × 192 in.
(244 × 366 × 488 cm); figures 68 × 38 × 38 in.
(173 × 97 × 97 cm).
Courtesy of Sidney Janis Gallery, New York.

95. *Blue Girl in Front of Blue Doorway.*
1980.
Painted plaster and painted wood,
52 × 36 × 15 in. (132 × 91 × 38 cm).
Courtesy of Sidney Janis Gallery, New York.

96. *Body Fragment No. 1.* 1980.
Painted plaster, 22¼ × 14 in. (56 × 36 cm).
Collection of Herbert Kohl, Milwaukee,
Wisconsin.

97. *Cézanne Still Life No. 2.* 1981.
Painted plaster, wood and metal,
32 × 40 × 18½ in. (81 × 101 × 47 cm).
Courtesy of Sidney Janis Gallery, New York.

98. *Cézanne Still Life No. 3.* 1981.
Painted plaster, wood and metal,
24 × 40 × 27½ in. (61 × 102 × 70 cm).
Courtesy of Sidney Janis Gallery, New York.

99. *Three Bathers with Birch Tree.* 1980.
Plaster and wood, 72 × 64 × 14 in.
(183 × 163 × 36 cm).
Collection of Michael Gregory, Wayne,
New Jersey.

100. *Cézanne Still Life No. 4.* 1981.
Painted plaster, wood and metal,
57 × 48 × 24 in. (145 × 122 × 61 cm).
Courtesy of Sidney Janis Gallery, New York.

101. *Woman Eating Apple.* 1981.
Painted plaster and wood, 38 × 38 × 8 in.
(97 × 97 × 20 cm).
Courtesy of Sidney Janis Gallery, New York.

102. *Helen with Apples II.* 1981.
Painted plaster, 96 × 48 × 42 in.
(244 × 121 × 107 cm).
Portland Museum of Art, Portland, Oregon.

103. *The Circus Flyers.* 1981.
Plaster, wire and rope, 72 × 144 × 20 in.
(183 × 366 × 51 cm).
Collection of James H. Binger, Minneapolis,
Minnesota, for Butler Square.

104. *Woman Standing in Blue Doorway.*
1981.
Painted plaster and wood, 82 × 55 × 33 in.
(208 × 140 × 84 cm).
Courtesy of Sidney Janis Gallery, New York.

105. *The Holocaust.* 1983.
Plaster and mixed media, 120 × 240 × 120 in.
(305 × 610 × 305 cm).
Courtesy of Sidney Janis Gallery, New York.

106. *Machine of the Year.* 1983.
(*Time* magazine cover)
Plaster, wood, plastic and mixed media,
96 × 144 × 96 in. (244 × 366 × 244 cm).
Collection of Time-Life Inc., New York.

107. *Rush Hour.* 1983.
Plaster, 96 × 96 × 192 in. (244 × 244 × 488 cm).
Courtesy of Sidney Janis Gallery, New York.

108. *Jacob and the Angels.* 1984.
Plaster, wood, plastic and rock,
132 × 144 × 76 in. (335 × 366 × 193 cm).
Courtesy of Sidney Janis Gallery, New York.

109. *Woman on Orange Bed.* 1984.
Painted plaster, 44 × 56 × 76 in.
(112 × 142 × 193 cm).
Courtesy of Sidney Janis Gallery, New York.

110. *Ruben's Women.* 1984.
Plaster and mixed media, 84 in.
high (213 cm).
Courtesy of Sidney Janis Gallery, New York.

111. *Portrait of Mayor Teddy Kolleck.*
1984.
Plaster and wood chair, 53 × 29 × 35 in.
(135 × 74 × 89 cm).
Courtesy of Sidney Janis Gallery, New York.

112. *Nude on Redwood Chaise.* 1985.
Painted plaster and mixed media,
35 × 67 × 37 in. (89 × 170 × 94 cm).
Courtesy of Sidney Janis Gallery, New York.

113. *The Constructors.* 1985 (work-in-
progress).
Plaster and mixed media, 13½ × 12 × 7 ft.
(4 × 3.5 × 2.13 m).
The Mary Roebling Building, State
Department of Commerce, Trenton,
New Jersey.

114. *Couple on Two Benches.* 1985.
Plaster and bench, 51 × 62 × 62 in.
(130 × 157 × 157 cm).
Courtesy of Sidney Janis Gallery, New York.

115. *Still Life with Pipe, Chair & Apples*
(Braque). 1985.
Plaster, wood, and paint, 42 × 57 × 6 in.
(107 × 145 × 15 cm).
Richard Gray Gallery, Chicago, Illinois.

116. *Still Life with Shoe & Rooster*
(Braque). 1986.
Plaster, wood and paint, 52 × 36½ × 27½ in.
(132 × 93 × 69 cm).
Courtesy of Sidney Janis Gallery, New York.

117. *Man with Guitar* (Picasso). 1986.
Plaster, wood and paint, 61 × 31 × 9 in.
(155 × 79 × 23 cm).
Courtesy of Sidney Janis Gallery, New York.

118. *Portrait of Jacob Javits.* 1986.
Painted plaster and wood, 96 × 44¼ × 43 in.
(244 × 112 × 109 cm).
Courtesy of Sidney Janis Gallery, New York.

119. *Couple Against Gray Brick Wall.* 1986.
Painted plaster and wood, 96 × 96 × 51 in.
(244 × 244 × 130 cm).
Courtesy of Sidney Janis Gallery, New York.

120. *Woman Seated on Chair with Caning.*
1987.
Plaster, wood and mixed media,
59 × 37 × 10 in. (150 × 94 × 25 cm).
Courtesy of Sidney Janis Gallery, New York.

121. *Lot's Wife.* 1987.
Plaster, and mixed media, 53 × 53 × 18 in.
(135 × 135 × 46 cm).
Courtesy of Sidney Janis Gallery, New York.

122. *Helen Against Wall with Door.* 1987.
Painted plaster and wood, 38 × 55 × 14 in.
(97 × 140 × 36 cm).
Courtesy of Sidney Janis Gallery, New York.

123. *The Expulsion.* 1986-1987.
Painted plaster, 126 × 144 × 84 in.
(320 × 366 × 213 cm).
Courtesy of Sidney Janis Gallery, New York.

124. *Abraham's Farewell to Ishmael.* 1987.
Painted plaster, 102 × 78 × 78 in.
(259 × 198 × 198 cm).
Courtesy of Sidney Janis Gallery, New York.

125. *The Street.* 1987.
Painted plaster, wood, and mixed media, 8
ft. 6 in. × 26 ft. × 6 ft. (2.59 × 7.92 × 1.83 m).
Courtesy of Sidney Janis Gallery, New York.